World Un

The World Unive   Library is an international series
of books, each of which has been specially commissioned.
The authors are leading scientists and scholars from all over
the world who, in an age of increasing specialisation, see the
need for a broad, up-to-date presentation of their subject.
The aim is to provide authoritative introductory books for
students which will be of interest also to the general
reader. Publication of the series takes place in Britain,
France, Germany, Holland, Italy, Spain, Sweden and
the United States.

Medieval

Studies

Library

Frontispiece. Palm Sunday procession in the cloister of the abbey of
Sant' Anselmo, Rome.

David Knowles

Christian Monasticism

World University Library

McGraw-Hill Book Company
New York Toronto

© David Knowles 1969
Library of Congress Catalog Card Number; 68-25148
Phototypeset by BAS Printers Limited, Wallop, Hampshire, England
Printed by Officine Grafiche Arnoldo Mondadori, Verona, Italy.

Contents

List of maps

Foreword

The monastic life in its Christian form, though unfamiliar to many in the modern world, has existed almost as long as Christianity itself, and there are many ways in which it might be presented. Here the way of history has been chosen, showing the evolution from the first hermits of the Egyptian desert to the outward-looking abbeys of modern North America. The biological analogy of the word evolution must not be pressed too far, for time and again the monastic order has returned for refreshment to its source, but in monastic history, as in the 'origin of species', we can see members of a large family developing in various ways, while some retain many characteristics of their first parents. Thus throughout the ages there have been hermits not differing greatly from those of ancient Egypt, and monastic groups such as the Carthusians retain today the essential features of the early Palestinian *lavra* or group of hermit-cells with a communal centre of worship. On the other hand the middle ages saw the development of the great abbey, whose chief function was the liturgical service in choir, while in other parts of Europe monks were working, in large or small groups, as apostles to the heathen. Later still, teaching and writing became the common employment in a monastery. All these varieties of life have continued to the present day, and in the course of this book an attempt will be made to see what it is that unites them all as monks.

Monasticism, however, is only one form of the religious impulse of devotion and service which has endured throughout the centuries. In the eastern church it has remained virtually alone, but in the west, when population and the resources of education increased, a great company of religious orders sprang up – canons, friars and others – which retained some of the monastic framework, such as the vows, the set daily prayers and other practices, while abandoning much of the seclusion of the monks. Even in the modern world, the great international and intensely active Society of Jesus (the Jesuits) and the simple communities of Iona in Scotland or Taizé in

France are lineal descendants of the first monks even if, like human individuals, they may have many ancestors and may have explicitly renounced this element or that of their inheritance.

All these are of set purpose given little more than a mention in this book. To do justice to their ideals and achievements would demand at least another book of equal length. For a similar reason the orders and institutes of women have not been included. They too have had a long and varied story, and although for many centuries almost all nuns followed rules adapted from those composed for men, in what is called the modern world their numbers and the variety of their rules and occupations have exceeded those of all the monks and orders of men put together.

Leaving all these to some future historian, the present study follows the fortunes of those bodies that are counted as monastic by custom and general agreement in the eastern and western churches.

This book is based upon a long acquaintance with the monastic life and with its literature. The bibliography will show some of the books that lie behind its pages. I must acknowledge in particular my debt to two books that have guided my path in periods and regions with which I was least familiar. They are the *History of the Benedictine Order* by the late Dom Philibert Schmitz, and the *Précis d'histoire monastique* by Dom Patrice Cousin.

1 The first Christian monks

The word monk (from Greek *monos* = alone, solitary) both in its derivation and its origin signified one who lived alone, or apart from others. In its sense of a religious devotee the word is a Christian coinage of the early fourth century, restricted at first to an anchorite or hermit, but applied in a very short time to all who 'left the world', whether they lived alone or in community. In the course of centuries it became, in many languages at least, still wider in its application to all orders of monks and friars, but it remains properly applicable only to those who follow one of the rules traditionally recognised as monastic. In the Christian church monks as a class did not appear until the last decades of the third century. Religious devotees, called later by western writers 'monks', existed previously among the Buddhists, and have in more recent times been found in large numbers in India, China, Tibet and Japan. In addition to these there was also a Jewish sect, the Essenians, in existence in the century before the birth of Christ, and among its members may have been the community of Qumran, custodians of the so-called 'Dead Sea scrolls'. These latter may well have influenced the life of John the Baptist and some of the early disciples of Christ, but all the many endeavours of scholars to derive from any of these sources, as also from any extraneous source, the fully-fledged monasticism of the Christian church, have proved fruitless. While it is true to say that what we may agree to call the monastic life has appeared in several of the major religions of civilised man, and is therefore a common human response to deep moral and spiritual aspirations, it is equally true to say that it was the teaching of Christ, and not a previously existing institute, that aroused these aspirations in a new form, thus bringing into existence Christian monachism.

As a matter of history, the monastic life and its near relatives and dependents in the Christian church have stood out from the early fourth century to the present day as a vocation for those who wish to dedicate themselves to a deeper understanding and more thorough observance of the commands and counsels of Christ than is demanded by the simple profession of Christian faith. This conception of the Christian life as lived at different powers, so to say, by recognised groups or classes, though borne out by experience in other aspects of human life, has been and is still a matter of controversy. On the one hand, reformers of all kinds, whether early Montanists, medieval monks or later puritans, have endeavoured to apply to all Christians all, or at least many, of the characteristic ascetic and spiritual features of monasticism, while at the other extreme, the monastic life as such has been denounced as contrary to the spirit of Christian brotherhood and freedom. Leaving this controversy aside till we have seen the witness of the ages, we shall be concerned henceforth simply with Christian monasticism as it has in fact existed.

The time and place of its origin are not in question. The place was lower Egypt, and the time a year in the last decades of the third century; more precisely, an Egyptian church in AD 271. Antony, son of well-to-do Egyptian peasants, heard the words of Jesus read by a priest: 'If you will be perfect go, sell all thou hast and give to the poor, and come, follow me'.[1] He fulfilled the three-fold command and began to live alone, dedicating himself to a life of prayer and manual work. No doubt individuals had acted in a similar way before. Antony differed from them both in the determination and sanctity of a long life, and in his gift for inspiring and guiding others, the stream of imitators that soon became a flood, begging Antony to tell them the secret of his life.

It is natural to ask whether monasticism, whenever begun, was in reality a totally new form of Christian life, and why the great explosion should have taken place at the moment and in the region that have been indicated. The monastic vocation, seen either as a movement, or as the establishment of a recognisable way of life for a class of men, was certainly unknown in the Christian church before 271. This is the historical fact that disposes of all attempts to trace Christian monasticism to a Jewish or other eastern model. On the other hand, early apologists of monasticism were justified in holding that the spiritual ideal was as old as Christianity, and was based upon the teaching of Christ. They could point to the call of Jesus to the young man, already cited, and those other words in which he spoke of those who made themselves eunuchs for the kingdom of heaven.[2] These were undoubtedly calls to a life of chastity and poverty, implying in one who followed them an unusually strong and effective desire to imitate Christ; at the same time it is equally clear from other actions and words of Jesus that marriage and the ownership of property are consistent with the profession of Christianity. St Paul likewise exhorts both men and women to a life of chastity and spiritual poverty, while assuming that most will marry and own property.[3] It was indeed not long before individuals and groups of women were found, living among their fellow-Christians but with a firm determination to remain unmarried, and examples can soon be found of men living what was later to be called an eremitical life. These however were individuals or small gatherings; there was a class of virgins and widows but not one of monks.

For more than a century after Pentecost Christians formed small and fairly compact groups in cities and towns, regarded by others with distaste and suspicion, and when their numbers increased they were liable to persecution and spoliation, but these were far less universal and continuous than was later generally supposed. They were nevertheless sufficiently exacting to restrict membership of the church to serious believers, and to make of martyrdom, the supreme sacrifice of life, the height of a Christian's glory and his ideal of perfection.

Towards the middle of the third century, however, the threat of persecution had receded and the numbers of Christians had increased. Though persecution was to recur under Decius (249–52) and Diocletian (284–305) in a form fiercer than ever before, this was in a sense a desperate measure, and was immediately followed by the conversion of Constantine and the swift transformation of the Christian church from a persecuted and fervent sect into a ruling and rapidly increasing body, favoured and directed by the emperor, membership of which was a material advantage. In the sequel, the standards of life and the level of austerity were lowered and the Christian church became what it has in large measure remained ever since, a large body in which a few are exceptionally observant and devout, while many are sincere believers without any pretension to fervour, and a sizeable number, perhaps even a majority, are either on their way to losing the faith, or retain it in spite of a life which neither obeys in all respects the commands of Christ nor shares in the devotional and sacramental life of the church with regularity. Under such conditions there has always occurred a revolt of some or many against what seems to them prevailing laxity; they choose the narrow way which, in the words of Jesus, leads to eternal life.

If we ask further, why this movement took place in Egypt, we can only note that in Alexandria and the delta of the Nile there was a large Christian population living very near uninhabited land, with a climate that allowed an existence all the year round on a sparse diet in caves or primitive shelters. It is worth noting also that very soon monks were exempt from military service, taxes and certain forms of conscripted labour.

St Antony (251–356), after long years of solitary life and more than one move further into the desert, became in his later years a renowned master whose saintly life and wise counsel attracted innumerable disciples and visitors. His fame grew with his long life and was prolonged by the biography written soon after his death by the great archbishop Athanasius of Alexandria. This became not only a spiritual classic, but an exemplar for all subsequent hagiography for a thousand years, and contributed more than any other agency to the expansion of monastic life. Thus Antony, by his example, his manifest holiness and his teaching, through his disciples and the written account of his life, showed the possibility and the rich fruits in spiritual excellence of the hermit's life.

What may be called the golden age of Egyptian hermit life ran from c. 330 to c. 440. The first 'fathers of the desert' lived alone or by twos and threes in caves, huts or brick-built cells, supporting themselves on the produce of their vegetable patches and small fields, making baskets of palm fronds which they sold to visitors or agents for money with which to buy the other necessaries of life. Their time was spent in prayer, in work and in reading and memorising the scriptures; such a life, if it were to be satisfying and fruitful, demanded an uncommon degree of psychological stability and self-control. Their penances and fasts were canvassed by contemporaries and have been criticised by modern writers. Undoubtedly the motive of performing a feat or outbidding an acquaintance was sometimes present, but the element of severe physical and mental endurance, accepted as a spiritual discipline, was part of the early monastic climate, though we may make an allowance for the Coptic physique and mentality, and for the climate and economic background, so different from that of western experience.

The genius of Egypt for the monastic life was manifold. It was an easy step from the solitary life to a group of hermits meeting together daily or, more commonly, weekly for the celebration of the Eucharist and the mutual exchange of counsel and practical help. Less to be expected was the birth, within a few years of the first monk, of one who was to be the first master of the common life. Pachomius (286–346) was a convert from paganism as a young man, and after some years spent as a hermit felt the call to provide monastic life for the many. An organiser and administrator of the highest ability, he created with no preceding model a monastic congregation which had all the elements that were to be gradually rediscovered and applied by western founders many centuries later. Recruits came in hundreds, particularly from the lower classes of peasant and townsfolk, and Pachomius gave them a rule and an elaborate institute. Chastity and poverty were presupposed, and to these Pachomius added obedience in its specific form as a condition of community life. While the hermit obeyed an elder as one more spiritually wise and experienced, the Pachomian monk obeyed his superiors as the disposers of his life and energies, and regarded the consequent abandonment of personal choice as a spiritual gain of the first importance. Organisation and obedience implied sanctions, and the penal code of Pachomius was the first of a great family reaching from Egypt to the modern world. In daily life the regime of the monastery was moderate in comparison with that of the hermitage. Wine, meat and oil were banned, but fish, cheese, fruit and vegetables were allowed in addition to bread. The community prayer, made up of psalms and lessons, was not notably longer than the modern monastic office. Work was an essential feature of the life. The monasteries were small towns of a thousand or two thousand inhabitants; they were divided into houses of thirty or forty, in which the monks were grouped according to their skills or crafts – tailors, bakers, gardeners, and the rest – and surplus products were sold down the Nile to Alexandria. There was a special house for brethren in service as messengers and distributors. The monasteries were grouped as an 'order' under a single superior-general, Pachomius and his successors, who visited each monastery frequently and could transfer monks from one to another at will. Beneath them were the heads of monasteries, each with an assistant, who ruled over the heads of houses. Two general meetings were held yearly, at the monastery of Pachomius, one to celebrate Easter and share spiritual counsel, the other in August, when the heads of houses presented the yearly account.

Besides its legacy of institutions and examples of holiness the Egyptian monachism left to posterity a rich literature of the spiritual life. There were in the first place the recorded counsels of the famous anchorites, the 'sayings of the fathers' preserved in three different collections. These are for the most part short, pithy sentences, many of which have become commonplaces of the ascetic life. Then there is the *Lausiac History*, the outcome of a visit to Nitria and other monastic sites *c.* 400 by the Greek Palladius. Finally, there are the *Institutes* and *Conferences* of John Cassian, written 415–29. Cassian, a native of Scythia and the disciple in turn of John Chrysostom in Constantinople and Pope Leo the Great in Rome, lived for fifteen years among the anchorites and presented their doctrine in a series of chapters to the monks of Lérins and Provence. Scholars still disagree as to the fidelity with which Cassian reported, twenty years on, the long disquisitions to which he attaches the names of celebrated abbots. Not only are they written in a single eloquent style, but some of them embody doctrine and phrases of Evagrius of Pontus (345–99), and one is clearly a piece of controversy directed against the teaching of Augustine on the need for initial grace before good action. Nevertheless, they probably crystallise much of what Cassian had heard in Egypt and Syria, and in any case they became a classic without rival in the monastic west. Quotations abound in the rule of St Benedict, and the *Conferences* were read every night before compline in early medieval monasteries. They were a *vade mecum* of saints as different as Thomas Aquinas and Teresa of Avila.

The sayings of the fathers are mostly short paragraphs, recording a word or incident. Some tell of ascetical or spiritual prowess:

Once an old man came to another old man. And the second said to his disciple: 'Make us a little lentil broth, my son.' And he made it. 'Dip the

bread in it for us.' And he dipped it. And they went on with their godly
discourse till noon next day. Then the old man said to his disciple: 'Make us
a little lentil broth, my son.' He replied: 'I made it yesterday.' And so they
rose and ate their food.[4]

Others show an indifference to personal possession:

There was another remarkable thing about Abba John. If anyone came to
borrow something from him, he did not take it in his own hands and lend
it, but said: 'Come in, take what you need.' And when a borrower brought
anything back, John used to say: 'Put it back where you found it.' But if a
man borrowed something and did not bring it back, the old man said nothing
about it to him.[5]

A famous story shows the great Antony as a master of discretion:

A hunter happened to come through the brush and saw Abba Antony
talking gladly with the brothers, and was displeased. Antony said to him:
'Put an arrow in your bow, and draw it.' He did so. And he said: 'Draw it
further:' and he drew it. He said again: 'Draw it yet further:' and he drew it.
The hunter said to him: 'If I draw it too far, the bow will snap.' Abba Antony
answered: 'So it is with God's work. If we go to excess, the brothers quickly
become exhausted. It is sometimes best not to be rigid.'[6]

On occasion, the sayings can rise like a meteor:

Abba Lot went to Abba Joseph and said: 'Abba, as far as I can, I keep a
moderate rule, with a little fasting, and prayer, and meditation, and quiet:
and as far as I can I try to cleanse my heart of evil thoughts. What else should
I do?' Then the old man rose, and spread out his hands to heaven, and his
fingers shone like ten candles, and he said: 'If you will, you could become a
living flame.'[7]

While the sayings of the fathers are chiefly ascetical in tone, John
Cassian was the vehicle by which another powerful influence
reached the west. Among those who came from the Greek world to
join the monks of Egypt was Evagrius of Pontus. He had been
associated with Basil the Great and Gregory of Nazianzus, but he
was deeply impregnated with the teachings of Origen. In contrast to

the early fathers of the desert Evagrius was an intellectual, and he distilled from the doctrine of the great solitaries a system of mystical theology which, as conveyed by Cassian's reporting, was the basis for all subsequent spiritual teaching. While orthodox and profoundly wise in his development of the teaching of the fourth gospel as the code of the mystical unity of the purified soul with God, Evagrius, a Greek and a Neoplatonist, tended to over-emphasise the part played by the mind (as distinct from the will) in the preparation of the soul for mystical contemplation. His insistence on the need of moral indifference to external experiences and emotions (the 'apathy' of the Stoics) and of *intellectual* concentration upon the unseen divinity takes him sometimes into

the borderland between Neoplatonic and Christian contemplation which was to remain, largely through his agency, a troublesome legacy for medieval theologians. An eloquent passage in what Cassian reports as the counsel of abbot Moses will show both the strength and the ambiguity of Evagrius:

The end of our profession is the kingdom of God, but our immediate aim is purity of heart, without which it is impossible for anyone to attain that end. Anything therefore that can disturb the purity and tranquillity of our mind, however useful and even necessary it may seem, must be avoided as baneful. Our principal endeavour, the unshakable aim of our desire, must be that our mind may cleave always to God. Everything else, great though it be, must be accounted secondary, trifling and even harmful by comparison. For when the Lord said: 'Thou art solicitous and troubled about many things, but there is need of few, indeed only of one thing', he reckoned as the greatest good not

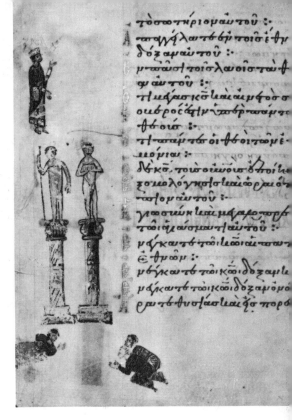

Left An example of Coptic (Egyptian) art. Christ with abbot Menas; a painting on wood from a monastery at Bawit, Egypt, dating from the sixth to the seventh century.

Right Sketches of pillar saints in the margin of a Greek manuscript in the British Museum. St Simeon the Stylite was the first of the class to become famous (389–459). Their feats of endurance, and their influence as counsellors and preachers, are in the main historically authentic.

the active life, though it abound in good and fruitful works, but the contemplation of himself, which is truly simple and unique. . . . It is impossible for a man hindered by the fragile body to cleave always to God and to be united with him inseparably in contemplation, but it behoves us to know whither to direct our soul's intent, and what aim the gaze of our mind should seek. When we can attain it, we may rejoice; when we are distracted from it we should sorrow, thinking that it is whoredom to depart for only a moment from looking at Christ.[8]

Pachomius, as we have seen, was moderate in his demands, and his disciples were legion. A reaction to this broad way was led by Shenouti (348–?453), an energetic, authoritarian, austere master, readily espousing causes and controversies, who helped to give to Coptic monachism its violent and tumultuary character in the fifth century. His significance in monastic history is his introduction of a

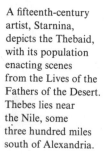

A fifteenth-century artist, Starnina, depicts the Thebaid, with its population enacting scenes from the Lives of the Fathers of the Desert. Thebes lies near the Nile, some three hundred miles south of Alexandria.

solemn promise of obedience, and his transformation of the Pachomian class of service-brethren into permanent servants, equivalent to the later lay-brothers.

Once in existence, monastic life spread rapidly and widely to Palestine and Syria. Palestine had its great pioneer in Hilarion (291–371), who lived as a hermit at Gaza for almost fifty years before travelling round the western Mediterranean in a vain attempt to escape from his clients. Monasteries were soon founded in the Holy Places and the arrival of Jerome and his group of noble Roman ladies attracted recruits. The mountainous desert east of Jerusalem proved as attractive to anchorites as that of Egypt, and the *lavra* (hermit-group) rather than the Pachomian cenobium (community) became the norm. In the *lavra* a number of caverns or huts at a distance from each other housed hermits under the direction of a saintly elder. They came together for the vigil of Saturday night, followed by the Eucharist, for a common meal, and for the allotment of provisions and material for work for the week. In Syria St Ephrem (306–73), theologian and poet, founded the

school of Edessa with a monastic framework of vowed students and the task of spiritual service for the surrounding hermits. It was Syria also that witnessed the appearance of the strange classes of solitaries chained to rocks either in a cave or the open air, and the still stranger 'stationary monks' who remained standing motionless either on the ground or on a pillar. Of these last the most celebrated was Symeon the elder (389–459), who remained for more than thirty years on his column thirty feet high near Antioch, a true saint who gave to those who pressed round his pedestal wise and temperate advice on spiritual and human problems.

Yet another outward form was given to the monastic life by St Basil the Great (329–79). Basil, whose period of study at Athens with his compatriot Gregory of Nazianzus has been made familiar by Newman, spent a year (357) visiting the monks of Egypt, Palestine and Syria before founding a monastery on his family estate. Though he departed from it when summoned to be a bishop he remained in actions and interest a monk. For Basil, the monastic life was a communal one, as giving the framework of a perfect Christian life of brotherly love and care, with the asceticism of service and humility, and penitence for sin. Liturgical prayer similar to that ordered by Pachomius framed a day of work and meditative reading. The work was agricultural and craft, but there was an orphanage attached to the monastery, together with a hospital and workshops for the unemployed poor. Basil wrote no rule and founded no order comparable to that of Pachomius. His so-called rules are spiritual counsels and commentaries on Scripture. Nevertheless his influence was great and lasting. By turning away from the hermit life and from individual feats of asceticism, he originated a monastic life that exactly suited the genius of Greek lands, and all the many monasteries of the Byzantine empire and indeed all the later monasteries of Russia look to him as patriarch much as western monks look to Benedict. Of Benedict nothing is known but his rule; from Basil we have everything but a rule.

Thus in a little more than a century Egypt and the countries bordering the eastern Mediterranean had given to the church the monastic life in all its essentials and in all its varied forms from the solitary life and the severely ascetic life, through the *lavra* and the 'reformed' Shenoutic house to the busy, moderate institute of Pachomius and the charitable works of Basil. A domestic framework, a detailed scheme of public prayer, a practical, ascetical guide and the machinery of an order had all been perfected, and in the saying of the fathers and the writings of Evagrius and Cassian had been laid down the main lines of a mystical theology that was to become traditional. All this had been accomplished in a little over a century. Those whose knowledge of monasticism is confined principally to the religious life of the dark and early middle ages can scarcely avoid the impression that the early monastic life was something rough, created among primitive peoples with a simple outlook and rude manners. A knowledge of monastic origins tells us that in fact the life evolved in the civilised

1 *The cradle of monasticism* The chief centres of monastic life in Egypt and Palestine, where hermits and organised communities lived in neighbouring districts. Antony's early and later retreats in the desert are shown, and the two chief foundations of Pachomius. Egyptian influence (purple arrow) on Palestine and Syria was at its height *c.* 400. Oxyrhynchus was the site where many biblical papyri have been found.

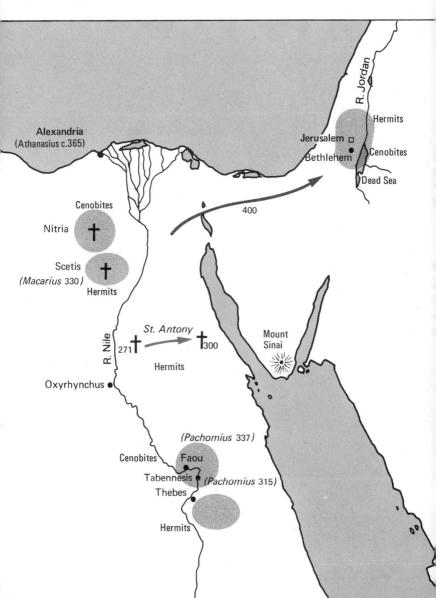

and sophisticated society of the later empire and found its leaders and its legislators among the ruling classes and the theologians. An eminent historian of the fourth century, M. Henri Marrou, has recently pointed out that of the dozen or so outstanding 'Fathers', Greek and Latin, of the fourth century, all save Ambrose were monks. This fact alone is evidence that monasticism, while in a true sense a flight from the world, is also profoundly Christian and catholic in its radiation. While in one aspect monasticism is the first great fragmentation of the 'image' of the single Christian family, seen from another angle it is an example of the inevitablity and value of development giving birth to a speciality of which the surplus can, so to say, be 'ploughed back' into the common store. But such reflections are artificial. The monk, as such, became what he was because of his intense and direct realisation that God is all in all, and that, in the phrase of a later saint, which recalls that of Evagrius, every thought turned away from him is wasted.[9]

2 Early monasticism in the west

Monasticism spread over the whole of the eastern half of the Roman empire in the last century of that empire's unity. There was no apostle to carry it to Italy and the west, no colonisation from the east and no action of bishops or civil rulers to introduce it. It spread gradually and sporadically as a plant spreads from seeds that are blown abroad. The most effective proselytising agent was Athanasius, who had been the friend of Antony and who spent the two first of his five terms of exile in the west. In the former of these he was at Trier (335–7), then the effective capital of the western empire, and in the second at Rome (339–46). He doubtless sang the praises of the Egyptian monks wherever he went, and his *Life of Antony* was a Christian classic in his lifetime. We can see the leaven working gradually in different circles: at Rome, where Jerome, secretary to Pope Damasus and already a monk at large, publicised the monastic life and formed a devoted group of great ladies who later (385) formed part of a monastic colony around him at Bethlehem and Jerusalem; at Trier (in all probability) Athanasius himself; and at Milan Ambrose the bishop planted monasteries. Augustine, to whom we owe a precious glimpse of these beginnings, adopted a monastic form of life for himself and his companions as if it were the natural result of a serious conversion, and when bishop he gathered his clergy round him in a quasi-monastic group. These two instances foreshadowed the later communities of canons in cathedrals and other churches, but they had no direct progeny. The so-called rule of St Augustine, an adaptation by a late fifth-century hand of the saint's letter of guidance to his sister's nuns, was followed by no community in the early middle ages.

The tide of monastic life swept most rapidly along the northern shores of the Mediterranean to Lérins and Marseilles (400–40), the former being the home of John Cassian, and here the inspiration came directly from the east. In Gaul in general, where the Roman civilisation, half Christianised, was coming to an end in an Indian

2 *The two streams of monastic influence* The purple lines show the attraction of the desert for Christians in the east (Palladius, Evagrius, Basil) and the west (Jerome and Cassian). The grey lines show the outgoing inspiration from Egypt: in the east to Palestine and thence to the Basilian monasteries and Constantinople; in the west through Athanasius and Augustine to Rome, Milan and north Africa, and through Cassian and Martin to Tours, west Gaul, Ireland, Cornwall and Wales.

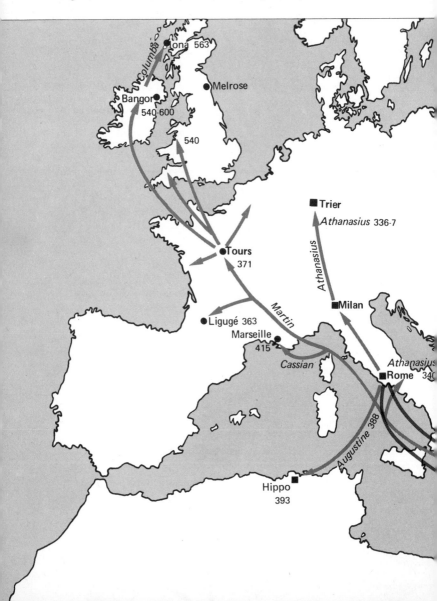

Iona 563

Melrose

Bangor
540-600

540

Trier

Athanasius 336-7

Athanasius

Tours
371

Milan

Martin

Ligugé 363

Marseille
415

Cassian

Athanasius
Rome 34(

Augustine 388

Hippo
393

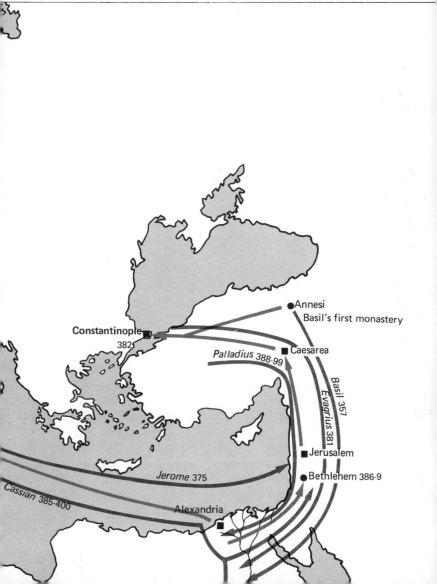

Annesi
Basil's first monastery

Constantinople
382

Palladius 388-99

Caesarea

Basil 357
Evagrius 381

Jerusalem

Bethlehem 386-9

Jerome 375

Cassian 385-400

Alexandria

Aerial view of Great Skellig rock, Co. Kerry, Ireland. This rock, eight miles from the mainland, here seen from the south with Valentia Island and the mountains by Dingle Bay in the distance, has ruins of three small churches and six beehive stone cells. The modern lighthouse is seen on the left.

summer of leisure and literature, the monks were regarded with dislike by many of the bishops and landowners. Nevertheless, the future was theirs. Towards the end of the fourth century Martin, bishop of Tours (d. 397), brought the life of a hermit-group first to Ligugé near Poitiers and then to the banks of the Loire at Marmoutier. Thence the monastic life spread fan-like over central and western Gaul, and from the west it passed, like the sparks of a forest fire and by a process unnoticed by chroniclers, to the Celtic regions of the British Isles. There, in Cornwall and Wales, and still more remarkably in Ireland, monasticism of a type radically

Virgin and Child from the Book of Kells, Ireland. Trinity
College, Dublin, MS 58. The ultimate provenance of this famous
work is still debatable; painted in the early ninth century,
probably in what is now West Scotland, it was brought to Kells,
perhaps from Iona by refugees from the early Viking invasions.

3 *Monastic missions before Charlemagne* The grey lines show the radiation of Celtic monasticism, chiefly between 560 and 670, to the Western Isles, Northumbria, Wales, Cornwall, west and central Gaul, Switzerland, south Germany and north Italy. The purple lines show the missionary radiation of Anglo-Saxon monks, chiefly between 690 and 760, to the Netherlands and west Germany, with the journeys of Boniface and Willibald to Rome.

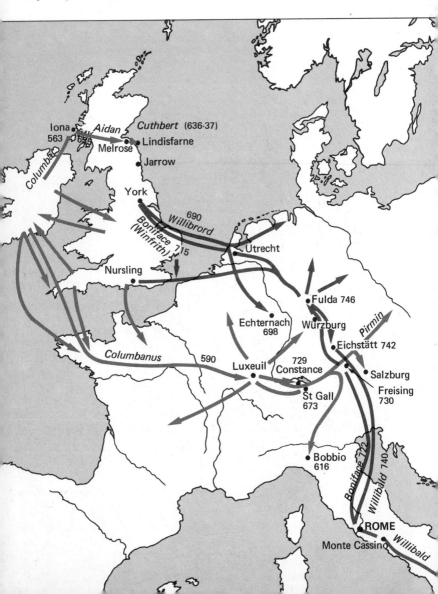

eremitical expanded rapidly from 540 to 600 and became the ruling element not only in the church but in society. In a land where cities and towns did not exist, and where the social units were the clan and tribe, monasticism when it captured the enthusiasm of a convert population rapidly became an epidemic. When the king or chief became a Christian he often became also a monk, taking with him the whole clan. In a large monastic community, sometimes two or three thousand strong, the king was often abbot. Regional bishops, established by St Patrick, were supplemented or superseded by abbots with monastic spheres of influence, and the functions requiring episcopal orders were carried out by one or more of the monks, consecrated for the purpose by order of the abbot. Celtic monasticism in its golden age was austere in the extreme; physical penances (some of which still form part of pilgrimages in Ireland) such as fasting and immersion in cold water, were severe. Yet at the same time, in primitive conditions that would seem to render mental exertion impossible, a vivid Latin culture sprang up and a still more remarkable artistic achievement that has put Celtic monastic illuminations and metalwork among the masterpieces of art-history. The illustrated manuscripts, such as the books of Kells and Durrow, the jewelry and the bronze bells and silver reliquaries, were made and used in wooden, wattle or dry-stone churches. Though the Irish monks could rival the Egyptian fathers, whose manner of life they certainly took as their model, the Celtic spirit was very different from the Coptic. We cannot imagine an eastern monk writing the following:

> I have a bothy [hut] in the wood,
> none knows it save the Lord, my God;
> one wall an ash, the other hazel,
> and a great fern makes the door.
>
> The doorposts are made of heather,
> and the lintel of honeysuckle;

> and wild forest all around
> yields mast for well-fed swine.
>
> This size my hut; the smallest thing;
> homestead amid well-trod paths;
> a woman (but blackbird clothed and seeming)
> warbles sweetly from its gable.[10]

Peculiar to Celtic monachism was its predilection for exile (*peregrinatio*) as a form of renunciation, by which monks took to foreign lands the Christian faith and the monastic life. Iceland, the western isles of Scotland, Brittany, central Europe as far east as Regensburg and Vienna and as far south as Bobbio in Lombardy, saw the establishments of the monks of Ireland (*Scotti*) who took with them their culture and their rule, embodied in paintings and manuscripts that survive in the museums and libraries of Europe. Foremost among these pilgrims in sanctity and influence were Columba (521–97) the founder of Iona and the apostle of western Scotland, and Columbanus (540–615) who left his native land and after several halts arrived in the Vosges mountains, where he founded Luxeuil (*c.* 590). Twenty years later, a series of adventures took him through the Rhineland and the Alps and he ended his days at Bobbio. Columbanus left a rule more austere than those of contemporary Mediterranean monachism, with severe fasts and a fierce penal code, but the heart of his monasticism was not a rule but an abbot, and throughout the family of monasteries founded or influenced by him the will of the abbot, expressed differently by different personalities, was the mainspring of the life. Meanwhile, by ways often invisible to historians, the monasteries of Lérins, of Marmoutier and of Luxeuil spread their teaching all over France and what is now known as the Low Countries.

Meanwhile hermits and small monasteries were multiplying in Italy. There was no organisation, no eminent leader and no influential rule, and the wandering monk was a common nuisance.

Most of the larger houses would probably have possessed copies of Jerome's Latin translation of the rule of Pachomius and Rufinus's of the 'rules' of Basil, as also the two great works of Cassian. In general, the abbot had autocratic power over such monks as were willing to stay with him, and we know from the anonymous *Rule of the Master* (*c.* 540) that the need existed and was recognised for a code which the abbot could apply as an approved norm. That rule shows us a small monastery of twelve monks and an abbot, carrying out a round of psalmody, work and reading, with a common dormitory in which the abbot's bed was in the middle open space of the room, and a common refectory in which his seat was distinguished from the rest. The life in such a house must have been as simple and as unadorned as that in the early Franciscan friaries. St Benedict, as we know, lived in and among monasteries of this type at Subiaco, and such must also have been the primitive community of Monte Cassino.

Benedict of Nursia (*c.* 480 – *c.* 547), regarded by all in the later middle ages and by historians and monks of the modern world as the patriarch and founder of all institutes of western monachism, held in his lifetime no more than the position of abbot in one of the many Italian monasteries of his day, even if he was renowned for his sanctity and reputation as a wonder-worker. He founded no order and made no mark in the church similar to that made by Pachomius or Basil or Columbanus. His fame and place in history are due solely to his short rule, and even this has been shown to be in all probability based upon the rule of the anonymous Master, his contemporary.[11]

Benedict's rule had no immediate celebrity. It was never imposed by authority and made its way slowly by virtue of its excellence. But even if we grant that some two-thirds of the text are taken from the Scriptures, the Master's rule, and other available sources, it is the rule of Benedict, and not any of those documents from which it borrowed material, that won its way into the monasteries of the whole of western Europe and is at the present day followed by thousands all over the world. It owes its triumph to three principal characteristics. First, it is eminently practical. Whereas the Master's rule is prolix and disorderly, Benedict's rule is short, and whereas other extant rules of the time touch on only a few aspects of monastic life this rule is a workable directory for all monastic activity and every class and age of monks. Secondly, while it is spiritually uncompromising it is physically moderate and flexible, and emphasis is laid on the charity and harmony of a simple life in common rather than on the rivalry and effort of individual achievement. Thirdly, it is unique among monastic rules in containing in a few pregnant paragraphs a fund of spiritual and human wisdom that can guide abbot and monks in all the vicissitudes of life. Benedict's monastery is neither a penitentiary nor a school of ascetic mountaineering, but a family, a home of those seeking God. A few extracts will perhaps show these qualities.

Ch. 2 and ch. 64: *of the abbot*. The abbot should remember always what he is and what name [*sc.* father] he bears, and know that to whom more is committed, from him more is demanded. Let him realise also what a hard and difficult task he has undertaken, to rule souls and to adapt himself to many different characters. This one he must praise, that one rebuke, another persuade, and according to each one's character and understanding he must adapt himself in sympathy so that he may not only not suffer loss in the flock entrusted to him, but may rejoice in their increase. Above all things let him not give his principal care to fleeting earthly things and so neglect or under-value the salvation of the souls committed to him. Rather let him always remember that it is souls that he has undertaken to direct and it is of these that he will have to give an account. . . . Let him study to be loved rather than feared. Let him not be impetuous or anxious, autocratic or obstinate, jealous or suspicious, for so he will never be at rest . . . and let him so temper all things that the strong may wish to follow, and the weak may not draw back.

Ch. 40: *the measure of drink*. Every man hath his proper gift of God, the one in this way, the other in that. We hesitate therefore when we have to decide how much others should eat or drink. Nevertheless, keeping in mind the weakness of the less robust, we think that half a pint of wine a day is sufficient for each. But those on whom God bestows the gift of abstinence must know that they will have a reward. But if local conditions, or work, or summer heats demand more, let the abbot decide, taking care that neither surfeit nor drunkenness result. We read, indeed, that wine is no drink for monks; but since nowadays monks cannot be persuaded of this, let us at least agree on this, that we drink sparingly and do not take our fill, for 'wine maketh even the wise to fall away'.

Ch. 52: *of the oratory of the monastery*. Let the oratory [i.e. the place of prayer] be what its name implies, and let nothing else be done or put there. When the Work of God is finished, all shall go out in absolute silence, with due reverence for God, so that if a brother wish to pray privately he may not be disturbed by another's thoughtlessness. And if at any time anyone wishes to pray by himself, let him go straight in and pray: not in a loud voice, but with a contrite and fervent heart.

Ch. 36: *of the sick*. The care of the sick shall come before and above all else, so that in very deed they may be served as Christ, for he himself said: 'I was sick, and ye visited me'; and 'What ye have done to one of these little ones, ye have done to me'.[12]

From the Master's rule, the rule of St Benedict and the *Dialogues* of St Gregory we can reconstruct the daily life of an Italian monastery of the sixth century. The monastery is a relatively small building of stone with a tiled or shingled roof, and around it are offices, outhouses and, at a distance, farm sheds. All rooms are on the ground floor and none is large, for dormitory and refectory and oratory need to give space for no more than fifteen monks. The oratory has a simple altar, and there are benches or stools of wood. Kitchen, novices' lodging and guesthouse are either separate or small appendages to the main block. There are no cloisters, but there are a work-room and a reading-room.

Every activity has the simplicity of a large family at work. The psalmody of the Office is chanted, and the lessons sung in monotone. There is no daily Mass, but Communion is distributed daily or on certain days by the abbot. The Sunday Mass ends the vigil begun on Saturday evening. Normally the night office begins at 2 a.m. Lauds follow at daybreak, Prime at 6 a.m., and Terce, Sext and None at three-hour intervals. Vespers are chanted in the last hour of daylight and Compline, for which no light is needed, after the evening meal and the short reading from Cassian that follows. In summer, from Easter to mid-September, and on Sundays throughout the year two meals are taken, the main meal at noon and the lesser at about 6 p.m. In the winter and on all fast-days there is a single meal, but a drink and a little bread are allowed in the evening. Between the offices there is reading or domestic or manual work.

The little community was indeed a Christian family apart from the world and with no interests outside its walls, save that of helping neighbours and travellers, materially and spiritually. Even within the walls there was no specific work. The monks at first were neither priests nor scholars, and there was no elaboration of chant or ritual in their oratory. They lived together to serve God and save their souls. We should not imagine them as resembling a modern Benedictine abbey in Europe or America; a closer analogy would be a small Carmelite convent or perhaps a community such as that of Taizé in the contemporary world. It is easy to see how a small house of this kind could go to pieces under an unspiritual or inefficient abbot; it is harder to imagine that its abbot could often be a man of the spiritual stature of Benedict or Cassian, or even of the abbot of the rule of the Master.

3 The Benedictine centuries:
the first expansion

The rule of St Benedict was written at a moment of change. The compendium of almost three centuries of monastic experience, it was to become the only code for monks during some six hundred years. Artificial as is all division of human history into periods, it is not altogether fanciful to say that between the birth and the death of Benedict Italy, at least, passed from the twilight of the ancient world into the darkness that preceded the dawn of medieval civilisation. In his boyhood the government and culture of Rome was still a shadow of the past; when he died, the Rome of the papal power was being born. The fragmentation of Europe, the disappearance of political and economic unity and control, the rift between the eastern empire and the western kingdoms were widening. In the chaos and turmoil of the age that followed, the monasteries of western Europe, from being places of withdrawal from a world that was seething with political and social activity, gradually became centres of light and life in a simple, static, semi-barbarian world, preserving and later diffusing what remained of ancient culture and spirituality. In the course of this process they became a part, indeed an integral and important part, of society and of its economy. While kingdoms changed hands and great estates were broken up, the monastery, self-supporting and self-sufficient, could often remain. It became a nucleus that could escape destruction when towns were destroyed, and that could receive gifts and prosper in times of peace.

In the two centuries between the age of Benedict (c. 550) and the rise of Charlemagne (770) the typical monastery of western Europe changed entirely both in outward appearance and in social significance. From being a small building housing a dozen or twenty men 'the world forgetting, by the world forgot', the monastery became a large complex built round one or more open courts and containing, besides a large church and the necessary accommodation for the monks, their novices and their infirm and elderly

members, offices for the administration and exploitation of large estates, guest-houses and rooms for servants and labourers. In its most extensive form, as in the monasteries of southern Germany and Burgundy, a monastery became a miniature civic centre, with almonry, hospital, school and halls for meetings of its dependents and civil and criminal lawsuits. Around it there often grew up a small borough composed entirely of those to whom it gave livelihood either by wages or by the purchase of goods. At the same time the church, from being the simple oratory of the Benedictine rule, was becoming a storehouse of relics and objects of art, visited by crowds of pilgrims, while in the cloister were stored illuminated service books, manuscripts and liturgical treasures. On the religious level also there had been a change. The early monks had gone into the desert and the mountains leaving behind them a highly developed urban Christian society with a traditional piety and observance. Now, in the wholly agrarian Europe west and north of Italy, Christian life was reduced to the simplicity of a small rural parish with a priest of peasant, if not servile, birth. The monastic life was both for men and women the only form of instructed, organised devotion. Consequently monks, from being a class of non-social individuals, became a class of 'twice-born' Christians, interceding for the rest of mankind with God and representing the only clear way of salvation. The majority were now in orders, at least by middle life, and were on the way to becoming a branch of the clerical estate. For such, manual work was unfitting, and the cloister, with its facilities for writing, reading, painting and artistic craft-work, became the centre of European cultural life. The liturgy was greatly increased in bulk and in solemnity, as the monks adored God vicariously for contemporaries 'in the world'. The 'monastic centuries' had begun. At the beginning of this epoch, as we have seen, monasteries deriving their inspiration from the east had varied customs of their own settled largely by their abbot, while those of the Celtic tradition had quite different practices embodying the rule of Columbanus, which was principally a penal code. Gradually the rule of St Benedict made its way, solely by reason of its practical and spiritual excellence, at first alongside other rules, later standing alone as the rule *par excellence*. As time went on, what had actually happened was forgotten and the myth grew up that all existing monasteries had in one way or another derived from the monastery of St Benedict. The legend of the mission of Maurus (St Maur) Benedict's disciple, to Glanfeuil-sur-Loire to become the father of monasticism in Gaul, was a projection of this myth. By the age of Charlemagne the position of the rule and of St Benedict had become so firmly established that the emperor could ask if any other rule was in use, and others could wonder if there had been monks at all in Europe before Benedict.

Meanwhile monasticism had reached northern Europe by another route. Pope Gregory the Great (590–604), himself a monk and biographer of Benedict, had sent monks from his own Roman monastery to carry the faith to England. There is no evidence, and little probability, that Gregory and his monks followed the rule of Benedict, and therefore no reason to suppose that they carried the rule with them to England, but they certainly introduced monasticism to England, and they were followed by other groups from the continent, especially from western Gaul. Almost a century later two leading men from Northumbria, Benet Biscop and Wilfrid, who had visited Rome and were familiar with Gallic monasteries, founded monasteries at Jarrow, Wearmouth and Ripon in what are now County Durham and Yorkshire. At Ripon Wilfrid introduced the rule of St Benedict, and at Biscop's monasteries we are told that it was one of several codes that he had brought back from Gaul. A monk of the second generation at Jarrow, Bede, whose monastery as he describes it closely resembles that of the rule of Monte

Cassino, became for all time the *beau idéal* of the Benedictine monk. Simple, calm, industrious, affectionate, devoting his whole life and his great gifts to teaching and writing while he followed the quiet liturgical round of a large monastic family, Bede, quite apart from his talents as writer and historian, can be seen as a personality of deep piety and singular charm, who wins the affections as well as the admiration of his readers. His own character may be read in his account of Eastorwine, a young abbot of Jarrow whom he had known:

He was a man of noble birth . . . the cousin of his own abbot Benedict [Biscop] . . . and he had been an attendant on King Ecgfrith, and had abandoned his temporal vocation and arms . . . He remained so humble and like the other brethren, that he took pleasure in threshing and winnowing, milking the ewes and cows, and employed himself in the bakehouse, the garden, the kitchen, and in all the other labours of the monastery. . . . When he attained to the name and dignity of abbot, he kept the same spirit; saying to all, according to the advice of a certain wise man, 'They have made thee a ruler; be not exalted, but be amongst them like one of them, gentle, affable and good to all.' Whenever occasion required, he punished offenders with regular discipline; but preferred, out of his natural habits of love, to warn them not to offend and cloud his cheerfulness. Often, when he went out on the business of the monastery, if he found the brethren working, he would join them and work with them, by taking the plough-handle, or handling the smith's hammer . . . For he was a young man of great strength and pleasant tone of voice, of a kind and bountiful disposition, and fair to look on. He ate of the same food as the other brethren, and in the same room: he slept in the same common room as he did before he was abbot . . . he passed the five days immediately before his death in a private room, from which he came out one day, and sitting in the open air, sent for all the brethren and gave to each of them the kiss of peace . . . He died on the seventh of March, in the night, as the brethren were leaving off the matin hymn.[13]

From Bede's monastic contemporaries in Northumbria and southern England a stream of missionaries went out to what are

First page of the gospel of St Matthew from the Lindisfarne
Gospels (Brit. Mus. MS Cotton Nero D IV), written by the monk
bishop Eadfrith shortly before 700 at Lindisfarne, the home of
St Cuthbert. In Northumbrian art and culture the strands of Celtic,
Mediterranean and Anglo-Saxon influence are woven together.

now the Low Countries and western Germany, taking with them
the rule of St Benedict and its monastic life. Chief among them were
Willibrord of Northumbria and Boniface of Devon, and their
followers founded abbeys, of which Fulda and Echternach were
the most celebrated. The evangelisation of Holland and Germany,
and later of Scandinavia and parts of Poland and Bohemia, by
monks was something new in European history. In all the countries
they entered the missionary leaders founded monasteries as *points
d'appui* and they were often the residence of a monk-bishop. The
German, Swiss and Austrian monasteries were indeed the most
complete examples of the abbey-county-town. Another form of
development was the abbey outside a diocese (the later *abbatia
nullius diocesis*) where the abbot appointed the clergy of the
proprietary churches on his abbey's lands, and had episcopal
jurisdiction over an enclave in the diocese, meeting the applica-
tions for consecrations and ordinations by applying to a neighbouring bishop for help. The letters of Boniface (680–755) are
unique among the sources of the evangelisation of Europe in showing the methods used and the personal relations of the missionaries
with their assistants and with friends left behind in England.

To all most reverend fellow-bishops, to venerable men in the white robes of
the priesthood, to deacons, canons, clerics, abbots and abbesses, set over the
true flock of Christ, to monks, humble and submissive before God, to
virgins consecrated and vowed to God and all the consecrated handmaids of
Christ, nay more, to all God-fearing catholics in common, sprung from the
stock and race of the English, a native of that same race, Boniface, also
called Wynfrith, legate of the universal church to the Germans and servant
of the apostolic see, greeting . . . We beseech your fraternal clemency to
deign to remember our insignificance in your prayers . . . 'that the word of the
Lord may run and be glorified' and to be eager to obtain by your holy prayers
that our God and Lord Jesus Christ, 'who will have all men to be saved and to
come to the knowledge of God', may turn to the catholic faith the hearts of

incipit euangelii
genelogia mathei

onginned   godspelles

LIBER

GENERATI

ONISIHU

XPIFILIIDAVIDFilii ab

the pagan Saxons . . . Have pity on them, for even they themselves are wont to say; 'We are of one blood and one bone'![14]

Thus by one means or another the face of western Europe by 800 was already starred with great abbeys. In Italy Monte Cassino, sacked by the Lombards late in the sixth century, was restored in 717; in France among a host of others were Ligugé (363), Marmoutier (372), Lérins (400–10), Dijon (*c.* 520), Reims (550), Luxeuil (590), St Denis of Paris (650), Fleury (631), St Ouen de Rouen (649), and Corbie (657). In German lands Echternach (708), Reichenau (724), Fulda (744), St Gall (750) and Corvey (822). In Great Britain Iona (563), Glastonbury (?), Canterbury (601), Peterborough (664), Wearmouth (674) and St Albans (790). These are only a few of the oldest and most famous. Such a list gives no impression at all of what may be called the 'monastic map of Europe', which would show abbeys scattered broadcast over every country, themselves possessed of estates and churches here and there in addition to the block of land around the monastery.

Among the many vast projects that occupied Charlemagne in the last decades of his life was that of reforming and unifying the monastic body throughout his dominions. Accepting the rule of Benedict as the only existing code he hoped to apply it everywhere, but he died before he had achieved his desire. The scheme was taken up by his son, Lewis the Pious. Uniformity was to be the norm of the operation. Besides the rule, a single elaborate disciplinary and liturgical code was to be applied, and an abbey, Inde or Corneli-münster, was founded near the court at Aachen, with the famous reformer Benedict of Aniane as abbot, where two monks from every abbey were to come for what might be called 'refresher courses' in the monastic life. The scheme was published and implemented at a great meeting of abbots and monks at Aachen in July 817; there Benedict provided a capitulary or agreed system of constitutions, and carefully selected visitors to ensure their observance.

The scheme failed, partly because the loose organisation of society in Carolingian times was incapable of creating and maintaining machinery for such a great undertaking, partly because the empire itself was shortly broken into parts and then dissolved into chaos. Nevertheless, there were lasting results. The project had created a myth which soon became a reality. By taking the rule as the sole code it implied that all monks had been and were still sons of St Benedict, and though the name 'Benedictine' was of much later origin, the phrases 'household (*familia*) of St Benedict' and 'sons of St Benedict' were currently used for the whole monastic body, and all looked to the saint as their father and patron. Moreover, by drawing up a code of observance and giving a commentary on the rule Benedict of Aniane had provided a norm, a document, to which future generations could and did return.

Quite apart from the activities of Lewis the Pious and Benedict of Aniane the monastic order in 850 had an 'image' greatly differing from that of eighty years before. During those eighty years there had taken place what has been called 'the Carolingian renaissance'. This was primarily the work of monks, and monks were its principal beneficiaries. Though in the eyes of its protagonist, Alcuin of York, it was a rebirth of ancient glory in literature and thought, in fact it was chiefly the development of an intense literary education in monasteries and cathedrals. Calligraphy and illumination became common skills, and the capacity to write elegant Latin prose and verse, and in consequence the ability to absorb the thought of the Latin fathers of the church, were widespread. The monks of the great abbeys of Gaul became an educated class, and if Alcuin was the schoolmaster of Frankland, a monk of the next generation, Rabanus Maurus of Fulda, was the schoolmaster of Germany.

The monks have rightly received credit for their industry and

Bird's-eye view of Cluny *circa* 1156, from a drawing by Dr K.J.Conant, whose reconstructions are based directly upon findings on the site. Left of Hugh's vast church (Cluny III) is the tower and apse of Cluny II (955–1000). The cloister garth was thus small and irregular. The large foreground complex is the infirmary and hospice, the latter built by Peter the Venerable.

sound judgment in multiplying manuscripts of the Latin classics and patristic writings. In a majority of cases the earliest and best manuscripts of these date from the revival of letters under Charlemagne and his immediate successors (*c.* 780–860), and but for that revival much of Latin literature might have disappeared. Less familiar and less spectacular was their service in preserving the heritage of ancient science of all kinds, medical, astronomical, botanical, biological and the rest, which owed its survival solely to the monastic scribes. Though much of it was antiquated as early as the thirteenth century by the fuller version of the same lore that arrived by way of the Arabs from Spain, and though all was finally superseded by subsequent advances of science, its value for the medieval centuries, and as a basis for later progress, must not be underestimated.

On the other hand, the monks must not be given greater credit than they deserve. They copied what they found to hand; they did little in the way of discovery or presentation; they often failed to appreciate what they found. Much of Caesar, Livy and Cicero remained unexploited in solitary book-cupboards, and monastic criticism failed to recognise the poetic value of Lucretius and Catullus. Moreover, through no fault of their own, they did nothing to transmit the Greek classics. The text of almost all the works of Plato was unknown; Aristotle's scientific and philosophical works, and some of the Greek medical and astronomical writers, came to Paris from the Arabs, while classical Greek literature arrived only in the fifteenth century.

Yet if the material was inherited, the form in which it was preserved was due to the monks. The manuscripts of the 'Carolingian renaissance' were written in the so-called Carolingian minuscule, which was in fact the elegant Northumbrian version of the late classical uncial, reduced in size, which was carried to the continent by Alcuin and diffused from his monastery at Tours. This beautiful

and extremely legible hand, which developed into the slightly more angular hand of the twelfth century, was responsible for preserving the texts from depravation, and has made their perusal an easy task for scholars. In addition to their work as copyists, the monks became superb illustrators, and the illuminations, as they are appropriately called, still glow with gold and bright colour that defies all modern attempts to reproduce its brilliance. For five centuries this was the principal medium for the painter's display of his powers; it was also the vehicle by which the art-forms of the classical age, of Byzantium, and of the east were carried across western Europe and fused with the Nordic and Celtic designs. The manuscripts served as pattern-books for the carver in ivory and the Romanesque sculptor and even in the thirteenth century, the golden age of Gothic sculpture, much of the iconography was derived from the illuminator's interpretation of late classical or early Christian art-forms.

Nevertheless, the sunlight of the Carolingian age was followed by the century which for Gaul-Frankland was the darkest of all

(850–950), when the empire fell into feudalism and monasteries decayed or were secularised. The year 909–10, when the abbey of Cluny was founded in Burgundy south of Dijon, is usually taken as the moment of birth for better things, but it was almost half a century before Cluny began to shape the monastic world. This great abbey, which, like so many others before and after, began simply as a new and fervent house, had the good fortune to be ruled by a succession of exceptionally able, holy and long-lived abbots. Odo (927–42), Maieul (943–94), Odilo (994–1049), Hugh the Great (1049–1109) and Peter the Venerable (1122–57), five great men, covered between them a span of two hundred and eleven years. Maieul, Odilo, Hugh and Peter were by birth aristocrats, and the friends and counsellors of emperors, kings, dukes and popes.

The status of Cluny was in one respect unique from the start. To protect it from lay or episcopal usurpation the founder had subjected it to the church of St Peter in Rome, i.e. to the papacy, as its 'own' church. This, while the papacy was for long in eclipse, was a purely negative protection, but when the age of reform and papal government began Cluny was well placed. It was no new thing for a skilled reforming abbot to be called in to deal with monasteries in difficulties, and already Odo became known over all western Europe as such a one. When Maieul died thirty-five monasteries had accepted an ill-defined suzerainty of Cluny; under Odilo the number rose to sixty-seven and the family became an organised body, the first of its kind in monastic Europe. The novelty of Cluny's treatment of her dependencies lay in the direct bond of monastic alliance and subjection. Each house founded, reformed, or accepted by Cluny, with very few exceptions, lost its abbatial status and its corporate independence. Its prior was appointed by the abbot of Cluny and all the monks took their vow of obedience to him. All were thus technically monks of Cluny, but in fact they continued to live in their own monastery. The bond with Cluny

4 *The radiation of Cluny and Lotharingian monasteries*, 909–1100 The purple lines show the expansion of the Cluniac network to Rome, Spain, north and central France and south and central Germany. Only a few houses of the vast empire can be shown, and it was not possible to indicate secondary lines of influence (e.g. from Fleury to England *c.* 950). The grey lines show the almost contemporary, but more limited, expansion of Brogne, Verdun and Gorze.

was twofold: the spiritual allegiance of the religious profession, and the legal – one might almost say feudal – link of the charter of incorporation, different in details in every case, which bound the dependent monastery to an acceptance of all Cluniac customs and disciplinary decrees. The abbot of Cluny was supreme, and there was no delegation or decentralisation. The dependency of Cluny was thus in a halfway house between autonomy and membership of an integrated order. In all normal everyday matters, both spiritual and economic, the prior ruled his community undisturbed, according to the manner of life of Cluny, but both he and they owed obedience to the abbot of Cluny and his community (of which they were technically members), and they had no rights or share in the government of the Cluniac family save as members of the domestic chapter of Cluny, which they rarely or never attended. They had the advantage of sharing in the privileges and the high esteem that the monastic observance of Cluny brought with it; they were exempt from disturbance at the hands of bishops and secular lords; and they had the protection of the Cluniac name. As individual houses, therefore, they escaped from some of the burdens of the feudal system. The disadvantages were the lack of independence, the inability to escape from the decline, when it came, of the great arch-abbey and, in the case of the English and other houses outside France, the disabilities of a technically 'alien' group when nationalities hardened. In the eleventh century, the moment of the greatest expansion, the principal motive for joining the network was no doubt the alliance with an establishment that for half-a-century or more was the religious centre of Christendom and the nursing-mother of bishops, cardinals and popes.

Cluny itself, expanding during Hugh's abbacy from sixty to three hundred monks, and with its church and monastic buildings enlarged again and again, ended by being the largest and most impressive monastic establishment in the west. Its church, as rebuilt by Hugh, was the culmination in splendour and magnitude of the Romanesque basilica, and it remained the largest church in Christendom until the sixteenth century, when St Peter's was given of set purpose a length surpassing it by a few feet. Refectory, dormitory and other monastic apartments were to scale, and the furniture and adornment were sumptuous. Although the opinion that Cluny was the power-house and the spearhead of the Gregorian reform has been effectively refuted, and the credit portioned out between the religious leaders of Lorraine and the strong company of individual monks, bishops and curial officials, the two abbots whose combined reigns overlapped the eleventh century at both ends were certainly men of European influence and connections. If Cluny as a body was uncommitted in the contest between empire and papacy, she undoubtedly controlled the greatest volume of spiritual influence in eleventh-century Europe, and as such stood on the side of the reformers in the matters of simony and clerical celibacy. The reforming papacy soon made use of Cluniacs as cardinals, legates and bishops, and for almost fifty years (1073–1119) the papal throne was occupied by six monks, of whom at least three were Cluniacs. While neither Cluny herself nor any of her major dependencies had any great share in the literary revival or the rebirth of dialectic and theology, Cluny herself and many of her dependents such as La Charité-sur-Loire, Moissac and Lewes were agents in the collection and diffusion of art-forms, either as patrons who amassed treasures of art or as founders who helped their smaller priories and proprietary churches to exhibit on a smaller scale a likeness to their mother church. Sculpture in particular and wall painting owed much to Cluny.

What was it, we may ask, that Cluny offered to attract such vast numbers to the monastic life? Once granted that nothing succeeds like success, and that the second and third generations of a great movement are largely made up of those who follow a popular cry, we may say that Cluny stood for the supreme development of the liturgical life on an unprecedented scale of regularity and magnificence. The monks of Cluny carried out what was then felt to be the *raison d'être* of the monastic order, the service and adoration and intercession for the whole of society, in the most superb setting and fashion. To be one of their number was a distinction such as is, in an army devoted to its drill, membership of the Brigade of Guards. From another point of view, in a Europe where peace and security depended upon firm and stable authority, Cluny stood for a fixed point of great stability, itself secure and able to protect others. It was besides the most majestic institution in the west, in an age when even the strongest popes were harassed by imperial armies and driven out of Rome by their own people.

Life at Cluny around the year 1050 had reached a degree of liturgical splendour unequalled before or since. It has been calculated that more than eight hours, excluding any private prayer, were spent in church and chapters on normal weekdays, and if at least eight hours be allowed for sleep and toilet and at least another hour for meals, it will be seen that the time available for reading and for such skills as copying and illuminating manuscripts must have been small. Manual labour was practically non-existent; occasional light garden work such as weeding or collecting vegetables and fruit took the form of a community exercise accompanied by psalmody. Contemporaries within and without the community bear witness to the exacting, almost breathless, round of offices, and to the various expedients, such as a manipulation of the chronometers to advance the hour and a system of relays of monks in choir, to fit in the liturgy and the numbers. In its heyday under Hugh, Cluny and its thousand daughters dominated the monastic scene. The task of the abbot was herculean, and though the machinery did at last break down the marvel is that it functioned at all and for so long. St Peter Damian, a strict reformer who would turn all monks into hermits, still was impressed by the piety and discipline of Cluny.

When I recall the strict and full daily life of your abbey, [he writes, after a visit], I recognise that it is the Holy Spirit that guides you. For you have such a crowded and continuous round of offices, such a long time spent in the choir service, that even in the days of midsummer, when daylight is longest, there is scarcely half-an-hour to be found, when the brethren can talk together in the cloister.[15]

Ulrich, himself a Cluniac, bears this out:

For often before all are seated in the cloister, and before anyone has uttered a word, the bell rings for vespers . . . After vespers, supper; after supper, the servers' meal; after the servers' meal, office of the dead; after that office, the reading of Cassian, and so straightway to compline.

And in another place he writes:

The numbers of the brethren have so grown that while they are making the offering at the two masses, while the kiss of peace is being given, while one is accusing another in chapter, while the crowds are being served in the refectory, a large part of the day goes.[16]

4 The Benedictine centuries: some reforms

In almost all short accounts of monastic history Cluny steals the show in the tenth century, but there were other centres of revival quite free from her influence. In England the monastic body which had produced Bede and Alcuin, the two great luminaries of the dark ages, and such missionaries as Boniface and Willibrord, was swept out of existence by the Viking invasions and the subsequent debasement of religious life. While the terms *monasterium* (minster) and *abbas* which recur in early charters may often be conventional titles surviving the reality, as in the names of modern country houses such as Newstead Abbey and the French use of *abbé*, they show how familiar the monastic life had become all over England in the days of Theodore of Canterbury and Bede. All reality had disappeared from this by the reign of Alfred (871–99), and though the great king was well aware that in his society monks were essential to the education of the country and the spiritual well-being of the realm, his attempts to revive the monastic life were a failure. The new birth took place almost fifty years later, and was in origin the work of individual reformers, though their efforts were ultimately crowned by the enthusiasm of King Edgar (957–75). The leaders were three saintly monks who all became bishops, Dunstan of Glastonbury becoming archbishop of Canterbury, Ethelwold of Abingdon bishop of Winchester, and Oswald of Ramsey bishop of Worcester and archbishop of York. Each of these men had the characteristics and loyalties of his native region, but each also had an intimate knowledge of fervent continental monasticism, and the life they set going was based on the rule of St Benedict, amplified by continental observance, and attuned to the needs and surroundings of the English realm which included both the old kingdom of Wessex and the Danelaw. Within half a century between the refoundation of Glastonbury (940) and the death of Dunstan (988) more than fifty fair-sized abbeys of men and women had been established, to remain as focal points of the monastic life for 600 years. Glastonbury, St Albans, Peterborough, Abingdon, Malmesbury, Winchester, Worcester, Evesham – all these and their peers, names familiar to all acquainted with English history and architecture – date from the revival of which Dunstan was the leader. They were the nucleus of what was to be the organised body of English Benedictine monks, and they were at their inception, and remained, autonomous houses, wholly independent of alien control short of the papacy. From the first they excelled in manuscript illumination, in the small fine arts such as ivory carving, and in musical composition and execution, but unlike the reforms of Cluny and Gorze they had a major part to play in the intellectual and ecclesiastical life of their country. They were the preachers, the writers and the schoolmasters of their age, their abbots were members of the great council, the Witanagemot, and from their ranks were drawn a large majority of the bishops of England between the reign of Edgar and the Conquest. The monastic revival was indeed only a part of a far wider revival in every department of cultural and ecclesiastical life. The painted manuscripts of the monastic cloisters rivalled the earlier masterpieces of Northumbrian art and influenced the cruder style of Norman work. The monastic churches, though doomed to replacement on a larger scale in a century, have been shown by recent excavation to have been larger and more elaborate in plan than had been expected. Moreover, the influence of monk-bishops zealous for reform was responsible for the introduction of monks as the choral body of the cathedral churches of Winchester, Worcester, Canterbury and perhaps Sherborne, with the bishop standing in the abbot's place. When, a century later, cathedral chapters were organised, with canonical rights of electing their bishop, the monks and their prior stood as chapter and dean, responsible for the fabric of the cathedral and claiming, often with success, their electoral rights even in the primatial church. In the tenth and eleventh centuries Dunstan, a

Drawing of Christ and a suppliant monk by St Dunstan (924–88) who revived Glastonbury abbey in 940 and re-established monasticism in England. He later became archbishop of Canterbury. The inscription above the kneeling figure reads: 'Merciful Christ I beseech thee to protect me, Dunstan. Suffer not the storms of Taenarus [hell] to engulf me'.

man of many talents, was also a much loved pastor, while Wulfstan of York and Aelfric of Evesham were among the masters of the Old English tongue. In the period of the Conquest another Wulfstan, prior and later bishop of Worcester lived on, a saintly survival, the only one of his countrymen to remain in favour with the Conqueror in an English bishopric.

A second centre was round the abbeys of Brogne, near Namur, and Gorze, near Metz, founded a few years after Cluny. Gorze in particular radiated its influence over Lorraine and south-west Germany. Its observance did not differ greatly from Cluny, for indeed all the non-Celtic monasteries of Europe had a common observance based ultimately upon that of Benedict of Aniane, with individual emphasis laid here and there. Gorze, however, never set up monastic or feudal bonds with its associates, nor did it display such a magnificence of architecture and liturgy. Unlike Cluny, it had no exemption from the diocese, and consequently found allies in the local bishops and landowners.

Yet a third centre was in the duchy of Normandy, where the Viking leaders, converted to Christianity, restored the abbeys sacked by their fathers and founded others. Here again the basic observance was similar to Cluny, and was derived particularly from Dijon, but two circumstances distinguished the Norman mona-chism from others. It was contained within the frontiers of an independent duchy, and from 1000 onwards under the close control of the duke, who in the middle decades of the eleventh century was William, later conqueror of England. Secondly, by a series of gifts of fortune, above all by the arrival of the two Lombards, Lanfranc and Anselm, it came to house a group of distinguished theologians and historians, as well as giving birth to many good abbots, and when, after the conquest of England, the Conqueror used his Norman monks to stiffen and reorganise the English monasteries, the mingling streams combined to form a

The figure represents Lanfranc, prior of Bec, abbot of
Caen and later archbishop of Canterbury. The manuscript
written in Normandy *circa* 1100, passed into the
possession of St Albans abbey, where Paul,
a nephew of Lanfranc, was abbot.

flood of talent, administrative and artistic and literary, that made
of the fifty years after the Conquest a notable era in English
monastic history.

The Norman abbey of Bec, indeed, the home of Lanfranc,
Anselm, Gundulf, Theobald and other eminent men, was one of
the summits of Benedictine monasticism. The life of liturgy and
learning, governed by a saint who was also the leading thinker of
his age, set an ideal to which monks of the seventeenth and nineteenth centuries looked back to as a model, and more than one
English abbey, such as St Albans or Winchester or Ely, came near
it in fervour for a time. In Italy Monte Cassino was enjoying a
revived prosperity. Economically sound, it was ruled by a series of
abbots who were at first patronised by the emperor, but later were
high in the councils of the reformed papacy, and its new church,
inspired by Cluny, and the notice taken of its deposit of classical
manuscripts, gave it an increased reputation.

The Norman Conquest, besides rejuvenating the Anglo-Saxon
monasteries, led to a great increase in the number of monks and
abbeys. Besides several new foundations, of which the Conqueror's
abbey of Battle was the first, and the priory of St Pancras at Lewes,
the first Cluniac house in England, was the most significant, the
Norman landowners vied with each other in founding small
priories, either to act as a body of chaplains for the family and
garrison at a large castle, or as centres of intercessory prayer on
their estates, thus creating the large, and on the whole unsatisfac-
tory, class of 'alien priories' manned by small groups of French
monks. In addition, six more monastic chapters were set up at
Durham, Norwich, Ely, Bath, Coventry and Rochester; this gave
to the monks control of more than half the cathedrals of England,
including three of the greatest. At the same time English monks
took the rule of St Benedict to Scotland.

Thus in all the countries of western Europe the black monks,[16a]

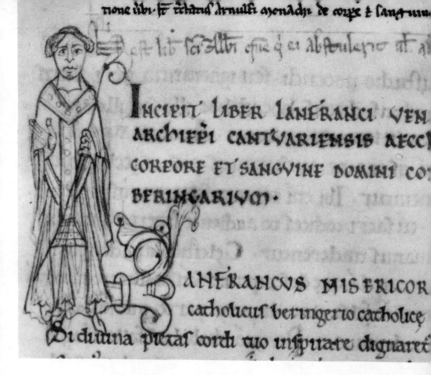

INCIPIT LIBER LANFRANCI VEN
ARCHIEPI CANTVARIENSIS AECC
CORPORE ET SANGVINE DOMINI CO
BERINGARIVM.

LANFRANCVS MISERICOR
catholicus beringerio catholice
Si diuina pietas cordi tuo inspirare dignaret

not yet known as Benedictines, were fairly established as landowners, administrators, bishops, writers and artists. A monastic
map of that date would show the long line of Cluniac churches
along the pilgrimage routes in northern Spain and their feeders
across France from Paris, Dijon and Toulouse. France was covered
with the dependencies of Cluny. In Flanders, the Low Countries
and the Rhineland were the abbeys reformed by Gorze and
Verdun at Ghent, Liège, Stavelot and Metz. In Switzerland and
south Germany the foundations of Columbanus and Boniface
were venerable bastions of church life, while in Italy newly reformed
Cluniac houses such as Farfa and the ancient abbeys of Monte
Cassino, Subiaco, and La Cava were, or were about to be, in new
life. The century-and-a-half between the accession of Odilo (1094)
and the death of Peter the Venerable (1156), abbots of Cluny, saw
the height of black monk ascendancy and achievement. The monks
had not yet lost their position of paramountcy in the religious,

liturgical and cultural life of Europe, and they had benefited by the rebirth in thought and letters that had occurred in the eleventh century. As historians, as theologians, as biblical commentators and as writers of spiritual instruction they were supreme until 1100 and still notable in 1150. Cluny, Bec, Moyenmoutier, Monte Cassino and St Albans were all in their different ways houses of unusual distinction, nurturing saints, scholars and administrators of the first order. Half the great sees of Europe and the papal legacies were filled by black monks, and indeed as agents in the Gregorian reform they were imposing at least part of their life on the whole church. In the letters of Anselm, Peter the Venerable and many others we can see men of high intelligence and holiness of

The abbey of St Albans, near London, founded in the late eighth century and refounded in the tenth, became after the Norman conquest one of the largest abbeys of England and renowned for literary and artistic work. Matthew Paris was monk here. Little remains of the abbey, but the church is mainly original, made with Roman bricks from Verulamium.

life directing others in the paths of salvation, and in the chronicles of Canterbury, St Albans, St Trond, St Benignus of Dijon and others we can see the daily life of great communities, with all their personal and administrative problems and collisions. Some of these abbeys, in particular Bec and Cluny, have remained ever since as exemplars for later ages to admire. The large, observant community with its liturgical, intellectual, artistic and civilised life differs considerably from the primitive simplicity of Benedict's rule or the Jarrow of Bede's day, but it is a valid development, and one to which many modern Benedictines have looked back with something akin to nostalgia.

5 The new orders of the eleventh century

Yet at the very moment of highest brilliance at Bec and Cluny an important turning-point in monastic history was approaching. The great age of medieval Europe's intellectual adolescence, which can be seen alike in the cathedral schools and the papal curia, is one facet only of the burgeoning of new life which is first visible in the monasteries. The families of Cluny and Gorze, the monasteries of Dunstan's England and the Conqueror's Normandy, were the earliest harbingers of revival and reform in western Europe. They were followed almost immediately by a second, less conservative movement, that of the hermits and ascetics.

The eremitical life in both its extreme and its modified form had been the ideal of early monachism, and had never been wholly neglected as the most perfect form of the monastic life. St Benedict, while emphatic on the virtues of the life in community, had nevertheless paid tribute to the vocation of the solitary, and hermits had continued to exist, even in Gaul and England. Now, at the end of the tenth century, the ideals of Egypt were once more to influence the west in an age of reform. In part, the reaction may have been due to the decadence of traditional monastic life in Italy; in part, the influence of the east and of Greek monachism may have been spread by exiles from the parts of the eastern empire that were being overrun by the Turks. The first celebrated name was certainly that of an austere Greek monk from Calabria, Nilus (*c.* 910–1005). He, and the Czech bishop Adalbert, soon to be the apostle of Bohemia (d. 997), were among the first reformers to visit and influence monks in or near Rome; Grottaferrata, still existing as a 'Basilian' monastery within sight of Rome, was founded by Nilus. He does not, however, stand out as one of the great leaders of reform. Here pride of place is taken by Romuald of Ravenna (*c.* 950–1027). Romuald left a Cluniac monastery with the declared desire of restoring the solitude and severity of Egyptian monasticism. His monument was the mountain 'desert' of Camaldolí near

The abbey of Grottaferrata near Frascati, on the slopes of
the Alban hills near Rome, was founded by the Greek St Nilus
of Calabria (d. 1005) and has always followed the Greek rite
and the so-called Basilian rule. The Romanesque church has
suffered a series of renovations, some of them misguided.

Arezzo, a congregation of hermits living in a *lavra* of small houses, meeting only for liturgical prayer and occasional common meals. Himself nurtured on the rule of St Benedict, with its familiar, if ambiguous, reference to the eremitical life as the crown of cenobitical training,[17] he founded a strict Benedictine monastery in the valley below Camaldolí, where years of training might prepare those who aspired to go up to the desert. A younger contemporary of Romuald, John Gualbert (*c.* 990–1073), like Romuald at first a Cluniac monk and later an inmate of Camaldolí, left the desert to found at Vallombrosa near Florence a strictly contemplative Benedictine monastery with perpetual silence and enclosure and no manual work. To preserve the monks from disturbance and minister to their needs he established a separate group of lay-brothers (*conversi*), and thus crystallised into a formal institute of great significance the occasional practice of numerous black monk abbeys of the day. A third name in the movement is that of Peter Damian (1006–72), who more than any other became its propagandist. Passing from Camaldolí to a hermitage and multiplying physical austerities, Damian, even more explicitly than Romuald, regarded the eremitical life as the only true life for a zealous Christian. He was summoned from the desert to promote by his acts and writings

The Hermitage of the Saviour at Camaldolí was established on a mountain six miles north of Arezzo some 2,200 feet above sea level. The monks live in small houses within an enclosure wall. They observe perpetual abstinence and almost perpetual silence, meeting together in the chapel for the liturgy.

the wide movement of reform that had now captured the papacy and the curia, and he more than any other gave it the monastic character it was to wear, while the institutes of Camaldolí and Vallombrosa remained small and hidden, though each has come down the centuries to the present day.

The spread of the eremitical vocation, as recent study has shown, was rapid and wide in the eleventh century, but it was also in individual cases necessarily impermanent. If the hermit became famous he was joined by disciples and the group, to preserve its cohesion, adopted the rule of St Benedict and the current monastic customs. Such was the origin of the celebrated abbey of Bec, and a few years later of Whitby and the revived Jarrow in the north of England. Such were the leaders, Vitalis and Bernard, of the groups on the boundary of Brittany and in Maine who founded the abbeys of Savigny and Tiron that grew into congregations with houses in Britain as well as in France. Two of these ventures have a significance above all others in monastic history. The founder of one was Bruno of Cologne, master and chancellor of the schools at Rheims, who abandoned a distinguished career in 1080 to join a group of hermits in the forest of Colan which included many of the future founders of Cîteaux. Leaving them, he was established with two companions by Hugh, bishop of Grenoble, in a remote site high in a mountain valley, soon to become celebrated as the Grande Chartreuse. Thence he was summoned to Rome, and ultimately retired to south Italy, where he died after establishing another group of hermits at Squillace.

His original settlement near Grenoble differed in no way from other groups, but it was saved from gradual extinction by an early prior, Guiges I, the friend of Bernard and Peter the Venerable. He attracted many recruits, and founded half-a-dozen similar groups for whom he codified the customs of the Chartreuse. These became and have remained with minor alterations the rule observed by the order, which was organised in 1176 with a system of general chapter and visitation, under the supervision of the prior of the Grande Chartreuse. The achievement of the Carthusians was to petrify or domesticate (whichever metaphor is preferred) the life of the desert. They resembled the Camaldolese, whom they may have consciously imitated, by living as hermits and meeting only at a few set times, but from the first their cells were built round a cloister to which the oratory was contiguous, and the whole complex was surrounded by a wall. They aspired to a renewal of the life of the fathers of the desert, under the cover of a semi-Benedictine observance, and thus to combine the life of a hermit and of a cenobite. The monks work, sleep, eat and pray in their houses, going to the oratory only for the night office, for Mass and for Vespers. In early days there was no daily Mass, and the life was one of solitude, silence and austerity, but the silence (unlike that of the later Trappists) was broken by necessary speech and occasional recreation, later standardised into a long weekly walk. Agricultural work was never part of their programme, and was not feasible at the Grande Chartreuse, but lighter employment such as carpentry, carving and (later) gardening was encouraged. Similarly, though the rule of enclosure was rigid, literary work based on the resources of the monastic library was not barred. In the event the Carthusians, alone of the eremitical orders, not only survived throughout the middle ages but actually showed a steady increase. Partly, no doubt, this was due to the cenobitic element in their life, which made a Carthusian house, even in a remote and savage neighbourhood, more viable than a group of cells; more, perhaps, it was due to the excellence of the customs, and the resolution with which all attempts to temper the wind to the shorn lamb, or to allow novices an easy passage, were successfully resisted. The Carthusians from the first had lay-brothers to provide service and craft work for the monks. At the Grande Chartreuse they lived lower down the mountain,

and the separate establishment was long maintained in rural Charterhouses, as, e.g., at Witham, Hinton and Beauvale in England. From the beginning the Carthusians enjoyed a modest celebrity, a *succès d'estime*, but they could not, and did not wish, to multiply and become influential.

That destiny was reserved for another group of hermits, who gathered in the Burgundian forest of Colan. Like the other ventures we have mentioned, they founded a strict monastery on traditional lines at Molesme, but in a short time benefactions and numerous recruits brought relaxation and feudal ties, and a group of twenty, which included many of the hermits of Colan, resolved to make yet another fresh start. This time their aim was to combine solitude and poverty with the severity of a life lived in the exact observance of the rule. The story of this move, which was to have such vital, if unforeseen, importance in the history of western monasticism, is succinctly described, with full documentation, in a group of sources that have from that day to this inspired generations of monks and supplied historians with ample material. Within the last thirty years, however, they have come under searching criticism, and although all the circumstances of their composition are not yet clear, it seems certain that in their present form they are the end-product of a process of growth, during which controversial motives may have led to the manipulation of genuine documents. This, however, does not essentially change the main features of the story, which we may read in their (alleged) own words:

They were twenty-one monks who joyfully proceeded from Molesme to the desert called Cîteaux, a spot situated in the diocese of Chalon which was at that time almost inaccessible by reason of thickets and thorns, and was inhabited only by wild beasts. Thither came the men of God, persuaded that that was the site which they had long desired, and which they now thought all the more suitable by reason of its inaccessibility and unattractiveness to anyone save themselves. There they cut down the trees and brambles and began to build a monastery. For these men while at Molesme had often spoken among themselves with bitterness and sorrow, through God's grace, of their transgressions of the rule of St Benedict. They saw that they and other monks had promised at solemn profession to keep this rule, and had in fact not kept it at all, and had therefore knowingly committed the sin of perjury, and so, as has been related, by authority of the legate of the apostolic see they had come to this solitude, that they might keep the rule and their vows[18]

The group of exiles from Molesme, thus settled in a 'desert' among woodland and marsh south-west of Dijon, began to live a simple monastic life according to the rule. This both they themselves and others before them had already tried to do, but the monks of the 'new monastery' as they called it were resolved that relaxation should not catch up with them a second time. Not content with present zeal and good resolutions, they provided themselves not only with a scheme of life, but with a clear programme and a constitutional framework. Before considering these it may be well to discover from the contemporary scene what were their problems and ideals.

The exit from Molesme to Cîteaux took place in 1098, and we have seen that the second half of the eleventh century was a golden age of traditional monachism in which not only the vast Cluniac family, but also the traditional autonomous abbeys of Italy, Normandy, the Rhineland and England were to all appearances in a flourishing condition. In some measure, therefore, the Cistercians were one wave of a great tide rather than an opposing current. Nevertheless, the luxuriant foliage of contemporary monastic life, which many might compare with a fruitful August, was showing, and in part perhaps concealing, signs of a coming autumn of decay. These were visible in several aspects of its life. First and foremost, as in all moments of monastic decline, there was an excessive involvement with the world. Separation from the world and from the spirit of material gain and self-indulgence are of the essence of monasticism. Now for more than a century of comparative peace and demographical and economic expansion, the monasteries had been adding to their possessions by purchase and gift, and to their capital value by careful exploitation. Concurrently, they had become more and more a part of society. Their own administrative activities and the link of feudal service were taking abbots and priors outside their monasteries and bringing founders and benefactors and royal agents – to say nothing of visitors and pilgrims – more and more into the monastic precinct. From being an enclave of seclusion the monasteries had become secularised, as much a part of their world as were the parish and cathedral clergy. At the same time they had gradually lost the traditional balance of the threefold division of occupation between prayer,

5 *Growth-points of Burgundy 909–1115* The map shows what influential monastic movements radiated from a small area of Burgundy. Cluny inspired Dijon, whence came the spiritual doctrine of Norman monachism. Cîteaux and her four 'elder daughters', La Ferté, Pontigny, Clairvaux (St Bernard) and Morimond, gave birth to the five great families of the Cistercian order. The cradle of the Carthusians lay somewhat to the south.

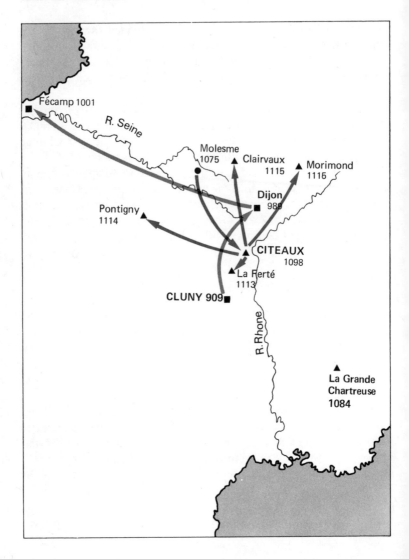

reading (or study) and manual work. The last had almost disappeared and the first had proliferated. Masses had been introduced and duplicated, the chant was more elaborate and prolonged, and a whole series of vocal prayers had been added to the office – offices of the Blessed Virgin, of All Saints, and of the dead; the gradual psalms, the penitential psalms, litanies and prayers – and all these changes had doubled the hours spent in choir. This had a twofold ill effect. It divided the community into two classes: the officials and the 'monks of the cloister'. The former were exempt from some at least of common duties; the latter, occupied for long hours in choir, were restricted to short periods of writing and reading in the cloister. Finally, the difficulties and the open spaces of the rule had been clogged by customs, many of them softening the severity of the original text. In a large community, with many members who have known the house for fifty years, it is extraordinarily difficult to cut away a privilege or change a dispensation. In a monastery, as in an army, the pace is the pace of the slowest regiment.

The age had now attained to intellectual adolescence and self-criticism, and the first Cistercians were not the only ones to see all these things. They were, however, a group of men exceptionally sharp-sighted in things of the spirit, and they were resolved to renew the monastic life. There is at present a difference of opinion among monastic historians as to their prime aim. Was it a protest, a revolt, a reform, or was it simply and only an alternative version of the monastic life? At the time and in the eyes of many historians of the past the general opinion was that the Cistercian movement was in origin and essence a move from relaxation to discipline, from failure to keep the rule to its observance, from indulgence to evangelical purity. Very recently, in the intensive historical activity of monastic historians, another opinion has grown up and is perhaps in the ascendant today. This holds that the first Cistercians,

Initial Q ('Quia amici beati Job') from the
manuscript of *Moralia* of St Gregory, an early
twelfth-century Cistercian manuscript from
the Public Library of Dijon. Note
the original brown Cistercian habit.

while admitting the validity and appeal of a monastic life which
aimed at sanctifying human values and using created beauty as a
means to an end in the service of God, nevertheless chose for themselves a way of abnegation and extreme simplicity. It was only (so
the argument runs) when the youthful St Bernard, with his brilliant
literary gifts and his puritan zeal, hurled at the Cluniacs and others
every stone he could lay hands on, that the black monks were
represented as a less perfect, indeed an imperfect, body of monks.
This outlook, which derives much of its attraction from the arguments of the great Cluniac, Peter the Venerable, is undoubtedly a
correct interpretation of the Cistercian programme of many subsequent centuries. In the centuries that followed, the Cistercians
were not to have a monopoly of fervour, nor the black monks one
of decadence. But at the moment of crisis in 1098 all the sources,
and the experience that can aid an historian to interpret them,
declare that for the first fathers of Cîteaux it was a question of
right or wrong, salvation or loss, and that they were convinced that
the way of life at Molesme did not permit of their living the life of
the gospel that they had vowed to follow.

The first task of the monks of the new monastery therefore was
to define that evangelical life. They found a sure guide in the rule
accepted literally to the last dot (*ad apicem litterae*), a striking
anticipation of the battle-cry of St Francis of Assisi: 'The Rule
without water (*Regula sine glossa*)'. This they applied consistently
and ruthlessly to food, clothes, work, liturgical prayer, possessions
and occupations. The result was a great and salutary liberation.
They shed at once – or, rather, they kept at arm's length from the
start – all the shackles that clogged the movements of Cluny. The
accretions of litanies and prayers, the elaborations of chant and
ceremony went by the board, and immediately there was fresh air
in the time-table; they refused all feudal and economic ties with
society, and the abbot was once more the father of the com-

ag
ne
vo
de
duc
au
ret
ter
cto
ce
ba
ad
ta

AMILI BEAT
Iob nequaq̃ puersi ee potuerint ꝫ

munity, living for and with his monks; they restored the postulancy and the full year's noviciate of the rule, and the life became a spiritual vocation, not merely a profession. They restored hard manual labour and became industrious, self-supporting communities. In two important respects, however, the one negative the other positive, they silently innovated upon the rule. They discontinued the acceptance of child-oblates to be educated in the monastery and later accepted as monks. This practice was on the point of becoming less general (Cluny had very few children by 1100) with the rapid development of clerical and lay education at every level, but the Cistercians felt rightly that it was not an essential element of the rule. Still more important was the adoption and expansion of the class of lay-brother. Whatever may have been possible in St

Benedict's small monastery in fertile Italy, a large community could not subjugate and exploit a wide area of marsh and forest in Burgundy in what must have been, allowing for Sundays and festivals, at most a thirty-hour week for the choir monks. They had renounced serfs and could not afford to pay hired labourers; the solution was to employ vowed brothers who had simpler religious and intellectual needs, and the institute of lay-brothers was born, with 'illiterate' men whose prayer was the *Pater*, *Ave* and *Gloria*.

Originally the lay-brothers (*conversi*) were all housed within the monastic enclosure, but when abbeys multiplied, with wide stretches of moor, marsh and forest cropped by their beasts and separating their arable spaces, it was impossible, even with their elastic time-table, for the brothers to work the distant areas efficiently when tied to the refectory, dormitory and church of the mother-house. In consequence, the system of 'granges' was established. The grange, originally a barn or byre, came to denote also living quarters and chapel, and squads of lay-brothers in rotation spent weeks at home and out on granges. This economic deployment of labour, and the escape of all Cistercian lands from the restrictions and complications of manorial agriculture and tithes, was an agrarian revolution of some magnitude, which made it possible for the monks to bring marginal land under cultivation and to practise pastoral farming on a large scale. These advantages had the un-expected and perhaps undesirable result of bringing considerable wealth to the white monks, especially those endowed with large areas of moorland or downland that provided wide sheep-walks. All this, however, was in the womb of time when the first fathers planned their day at Cîteaux.

Their bold and wise decisions showed that they had in their midst farseeing and resolute leaders, though we have few personal details of any save the two who were in succession abbots, the Frenchman Alberic and the Englishman, sometime a boy in the cloister at Sherborne, Stephen Harding. For a number of years the fate of the new monastery hung in the balance, while poverty, austerity and illness thinned their ranks and discouraged recruits, but as so often happens in such enterprises, heroism and patience had their reward. Not only did postulants arrive, but among them was one endowed with a dynamic personality to which a parallel can scarcely be found even among the saints. The arrival of Bernard, with a large company of uncles, brothers, cousins and nephews, was a crucial moment in European as well as in Cistercian history, and the young monk, within four years the founding abbot of Clairvaux, was to enter upon a career of forty years in which he was unquestionably the most powerful force in Christendom.

Growth of numbers at Cîteaux and the importunity of would-be founders led to the first dispersals of the monks of the new monastery. The first fathers knew well how soon spiritual strength is lost when tradition weakens, and they had in Stephen Harding a statesman with a clear mind. Adopting and blending old monastic and canonical decrees that had for centuries been obsolete, he embodied them in the first edition of the celebrated Charter of Charity (*Carta Caritatis*), that freely-forged bond between mother and daughter that was to take the place of the formal charter of dependence issued by Cluny to one who joined her family. In this the daughter abbey undertook to imitate and perpetuate in every respect, material and spiritual, the observance and discipline of Cîteaux. Beyond this, two safeguards unknown to contemporary monachism were imposed. The one was the system of visitation, by which the daughter abbey was 'visited' every year by the abbot of the founding mother, who examined abbot and monks on every point according to the rule, the *Carta Caritatis* and subsequent statutes, with full powers of correction and punishment. The other was the annual general chapter. This began as an annual visit of the abbot of the daughter house to the conventual (daily) chapter of faults at

Cîteaux, the formal disciplinary meeting of the monks. In this the visiting abbot could accuse himself, or be accused by others, of faults against the Cistercian way of life. As the order grew this informal meeting became impracticable and was changed by stages into a solemn gathering at Cîteaux in September, confined to the abbots of the order, who then formed a judicial and legislative body to adjudicate disputes and difficult cases, authorise foundations, and pass statutes for the whole order. Thus gradually the logic of events turned an easy family relationship into a closely knit religious order, the first of its kind in the church. Yet while its organisation hardened into a canonical mould, Cîteaux remained true to its abhorrence of the imperial claims of Cluny. General

Apparition of St Malachy to St Bernard, by the
Master of Palma de Mallorca, *circa* 1290. Malachy,
archbishop of Armagh, was a personal friend of
Bernard, who wrote his life story. He retired to
Clairvaux, to die there in 1148.

77

chapters took place always at Cîteaux, but the abbot of that house was no more than *primus inter pares*, the host and chairman of the gathering in the well loved nursery of the order.

The first foundation, La Ferté, was made in 1115 and in the same year Clairvaux began its career. When Bernard died in 1153, the order numbered three hundred and thirty-nine houses, of which Clairvaux had founded no less than sixty-eight, from which had sprung another ninety-one. At the same moment the British Isles contained one hundred and twenty-two abbeys, Italy eighty-eight, Spain fifty-six and the German-speaking lands more than one hundred. A halt was called officially in 1155, but it was never fully effective, and in the fifteenth century there were more than seven hundred Cistercian abbeys of men and nine hundred nunneries.

Such an explosion of monachism needs an explanation, even at the peak of the age of faith. Several causes of different kinds may be suggested. There was, in the first place, the demographic-economic cause. The population of Europe was rapidly expanding, and probably doubled between 1050 and 1200 which, all things being equal, would imply a similar increase in all main categories of the population. This growth also set up a pressure on marginal lands, and here the Cistercians who chose remote spots and had a mobile labour force were in a strong position. Then the century 1050 – 1150 was pre-eminently the monastic century *par excellence* in which the life called all serious Christians as never before or since, and here the Cistercians, with choir monks and lay-brothers, catered for a far larger bracket of society than any other institute. Then there was the simplicity, the thoroughness of the Cistercian ideal, and the excellence of its simple but inclusive constitution which seemed to guarantee a life of fervour. Finally there was the saintly personality of St Bernard, one of the small class of supremely great men whose gifts and opportunities have been exactly matched. As a leader, as a writer, as a preacher and as a saint his personal magnetism and his spiritual power were far-reaching and irresistible. Men came from the ends of Europe to Clairvaux, and were sent out again all over the continent, and after all her foundations the abbey still held 700 monks. For forty years Cîteaux-Clairvaux was the spiritual centre of Europe, and at one time St Bernard had among his ex-monks the pope, the archbishop of York, and cardinals and bishops in plenty.

We cannot indeed say how much the expansion of Cîteaux was due to Bernard's presence, but it is safe to hazard a guess that without him the order would have remained relatively small, perhaps half its actual size. The mistake made by many of considering him the founder of the Cistercians (who indeed were known at one time as Bernardines) is in some ways a happy one. Yet at the same time Bernard influenced the order in two ways not altogether for its greater good. In the first place it seems certain that the puritanical, fiercely anti-aesthetic note heard and seen in early Cistercian writings is not the voice of the first fathers. Theirs was the simplicity of poor men, but they accepted and indeed created beauty when they could. It was only later, when Bernard, now attaining celebrity and with a solid following of his sons in general chapter, could sway deliberations that the statutes imposing meanness and plainness rather than simplicity were passed and they had in fact no long life of full observance, though they have exerted their influence again and again through the ages. Secondly – and almost in contradiction to this – Bernard, by reason of his gifts, the circumstances of his life and the calls made upon him, became influential in word and work far outside the walls of his monastery. The first fathers had chosen to be hidden and silent; Bernard was neither, and his example, so powerful and so enduring, could not be obliterated. From his day onwards in the middle ages, with William of St Thierry, Ailred of Rievaulx, Adam of Lille and an army of Cistercian cardinals and bishops, the white monks worked upon the world by voice, by pen and by action.

Whether or no the first fathers had left Molesme because of its monastic decadence, they certainly had no intention of publicising their grievances. They asked only to live their own way of life apart from and unknown to the world. But when, twenty years later, Cîteaux had begun to multiply and make foundations they inevitably appeared as rivals and critics of the traditional monasticism. The mere fact that they claimed to follow exactly the rule, that both they and the black monks professed, was enough to cause friction, and a small incident touched off a great controversy which soon became one of the major debates in monastic history, and one reaching to the depths of the spiritual life, in which each reader finds himself drawn to one side or the other, in some such way as the student of thought feels himself insensibly attracted either to the teaching of Plato or to that of Aristotle. What might have been a smouldering and tedious wrangle was lifted to the level of a perennial division of ideals by the character and genius of the spokesman for either side. The incident that started the warfare was in itself a personal, insignificant matter. Bernard in his first years as abbot of Clairvaux had among his monks a young relative whose parents had in his childhood promised him to Cluny. The going at Clairvaux proved too hard for him, and he fled to Cluny, where the grand prior made much of the prodigal. Bernard, injured both as a man and as a monk, wrote him a passionate letter, which he undoubtedly hoped would circulate at Cluny, in which he compared the pleasant, easy, luxurious life in the great abbey with the spare diet and hard living at Clairvaux. News of this came to the ears of the young abbot of Cluny, Peter, later to be known as the Venerable. Peter was an excellent foil to Bernard. While both were aristocrats, gifted rulers of men and zealous monks, Peter was conciliatory, moderate, gentle, considerate and conservative, while Bernard was ardent, provocative, violent, uncompromising and revolutionary.

While Peter preached discretion and charity, Bernard demanded truth and sacrifice. Peter defended the Cluniac way of life as one that condescended to human weakness and mitigated rules in order that souls might be saved; Bernard retorted by repeating the demands of Christ which surpassed the claims of merely human discretion, and instanced the monks and saints of past ages and the clear commands of the rule. Then, intoxicated by his own rhetoric, he proceeded to give a highly coloured panorama of Cluniac life with a searing indictment of its monastic degeneracy. The battle continued for long, but when at last the two met one another each realised the other's sincerity and nobility of character. Peter, by his earnest and sorrowful attempts to reform Cluny, admitted the truth of Bernard's strictures, while Bernard explicitly recognised the good faith and virtues of Peter; indeed, his title of 'venerable' occurs for the first time in one of Bernard's letters. Nevertheless, the controversy is

Abbot Suger (d. 1151) reformer, statesman and friend of St Bernard, rebuilt the abbey church of St Denis 1137–50 as the first complete example of the new 'Gothic' style, with statuary and stained glass, planned by the abbot himself. He is seen here, in a window of the choir, as a suppliant of the Virgin Mary.

still a living one, and in this shape or that will always live. While we may allow that Bernard confused ethics and aesthetics, condemning alike luxury and beauty, and demanded more than ordinary human beings can give, we may feel also that Peter gave the name of charity to indulgence, and failed (at least in his early utterances) to give to his monks a clear invitation to complete surrender to the call of Christ.

Historians of today are as divided in their opinions of Cluny and Cîteaux as were the contemporaries of the two great abbots. The magnificent architecture, sculpture and metalwork of the immense Cluniac churches, the splendours of their liturgy and chant, and the humane and moderate outlook of Peter the Venerable, display in the eyes of many the beauty of medieval holiness at its best. Suger, the eminent abbot of St Denis at Paris, wise statesman and incomparable patron of the arts, like Peter at first the target for Bernard's heaviest artillery and later the recipient of honeyed words of friendship, was not a Cluniac, but his interpretation of the rule and his attitude to art and precious things in relation to the service of God differed little from that of Cluny. Here, in the restricted field of aesthetics, he and Bernard joined in another controversy that is still a living one. For Suger beauty of colour and form, and in particular the beauty of light shining through glass or reflected from jewels, was the first step on the ladder that led to eternal light, God himself, and in building a house of God only the most precious, the most beautiful, was good enough. To Bernard all this is hypocrisy or at best a policy suited to laymen, not monks; for monks gold and precious stones are anathema; they pray to the invisible God without the aid – or the distraction – of things bright and beautiful. Here is Bernard, with memories of Cluny before his mind's eye:

I will not dwell upon the vast height of their churches, their unconscionable length, their preposterous breadth, their richly polished panelling, all of which distracts the eyes of the worshipper and hinders his devotion. You throw money into your decorations to make it breed. You spend for profit. Your bejewelled wheels (you call them 'crowns') set with lamps and as bright as flames, your candlesticks as tall as trees, great masses of bronze of exquisite workmanship, and as dazzling with their precious stones as the lights that surmount them, what, think you, is the purpose of all this? Will it melt a sinner's heart and not rather keep him gazing in wonder? O vanity of vanities – no, insanity rather than vanity![19]

And here is Suger:

There are those who tell us that a holy mind, a pure heart and a right intent suffice for the ministration of the altar, and I would grant that these are the principal, proper and peculiar qualifications. But I maintain that we should do homage also to the rite of the Holy Sacrifice, as to nothing else in the world, with the outward splendour of the holy vessels, with all inward purity and all outward magnificence.[20]

6 The monastic conquest

In the sequel, events were soon to make the arguments of both Bernard and Peter seem unreal. Though the first fifty years of the twelfth century saw the monastic ideal and the monastic body in a position of apparently unassailable supremacy in the medieval church, the deaths of the two great abbots (1153 and 1156) took place at a climacteric moment. Cluny and the traditional Benedictines had in fact lost out to the Cistercians on the one hand and to the infant universities on the other. Nor was that all. Within a decade or two all monks of whatever habit seemed to be losing not only some of their fervour, but also some of their individuality among the numerous new orders – Augustinian canons,[21a] Premonstratensian canons, Gilbertine canons, military orders and the rest, and very soon the friars were to come as a tidal wave submerging all.

But for a moment, a space of fifty years, monasticism seemed to have conquered the western church. In the dark ages, when the secular clergy and the bishops were very generally appointed and controlled by emperors, kings, magnates and landowners the monks had gradually gained a monopoly of learning and fervour. They had elaborated the liturgy and multiplied manuscripts of the fathers and spiritual writers, as well as of the poets and historians of Rome. When the great reform movement got under way it was manned and steered by monks, who gave as a nostrum for all spiritual ills the monastic virtues and devotions – chastity, obedience and the liturgy. At the extreme right wing was Peter Damian, who would gladly have led every devout Christian into a hermitage, but others from Gregory vii to Eugenius iii, from Anselm to Bernard, could only give what they themselves had, the monastic ascetic and spiritual programme. Thus the whole church was monachised in various degrees. The clergy were brought back to celibacy and a serious attempt was made to direct all of them into a canonical, communal form of life, with the main features of monasticism. Devout lay-folk, if they could not or would not become monks or nuns, were exhorted to say the short office of the Blessed Virgin and, if no longer hindered by a husband or wife, to end their days in the infirmary of a monastery or nunnery clothed with the monastic habit to help them heavenwards (*ad succurrendum*). St Bernard and others invited, begged and almost bullied their lay friends to take refuge in the secure haven of Cîteaux or Clairvaux. But in fact the world needed little pressing. As the current saying had it, the whole earth was becoming Cistercian, and in the institute of lay-brethren the white monks had opened their doors to a vast new class of the illiterate. Abbeys of 300 choir monks might have as many, or more, lay-brothers. Rievaulx in Yorkshire seems to have had almost five hundred, and Walter Daniel, Ailred's biographer, describes the church on feast days, when all were at home from the granges, as packed with monks and brothers as close as bees in a hive or the heaven of devout imagination with angels.

St Bernard, when asked to provide a rule for the new military orders, handed out the rule of St Benedict and the Cistercian customs, and the great crusading castles, such as Crac des Chevalliers in Palestine, showed itself as a fortress without, while within it was a monastery. On the level of liturgy, the monastic rites, developed from the ancient secular rites of Rome and Gaul, filtered back again to Rome to influence the missal and the breviary of the Roman church, adding hymns and antiphons and ceremonies. All subsequent liturgical reforms, such as that of the Counter-Reformation and that of today, are in fact largely concerned with stripping from the liturgy of the universal church the monastic accretions of the early middle ages; indeed at the present moment the pendulum has swung back across the line, and the monastic liturgy itself is losing some of its own characteristics in favour of uniformity.

In the forty years of Bernard's Cistercian life the white monks

The Cistercian abbey of Fountains, near Ripon (Yorkshire), was founded by reformers from St Mary's York, in 1132 and became one of the largest and wealthiest houses of the order. Here, the long building to the left is the lay-brothers' range: the white surface is the floor of their dormitory. The tower, prohibited by early statutes, was a late addition.

poured across Europe almost as speedily and even more ubiquitously than the armies of Napoleon. If the Cistercians never penetrated to Smolensk and Moscow, they reached the west of Ireland and the Moray Firth. The first colony in the British Isles came from L'Aumône to Waverley in Surrey in 1128, but the first to attract attention was the arrival under abbot William in 1132 of the founding community at Rievaulx near Helmsley in the North Riding of Yorkshire, soon to become the home of the best known, most gifted and most attractive of English white monks, the Northumbrian Ailred, the steward of King David I of Scotland and friend of his son, prince Henry.

Even before Ailred's arrival the leaven of Rievaulx had begun to work. In the large black monk abbey of St Mary's, York, the drama of Molesme and Cîteaux was being re-enacted. A group of unusually able men; several of whom were to become abbots, were dissatisfied with the level of the monastic life there, and begged the abbot to take action. He refused; a controversy which came near to being a riot took place, and the archbishop of York was called in as arbiter. Failing to make peace, he took the reformers away, and settled them on a parcel of his estates in Skeldale. There they began again in wooden huts which ultimately became the great abbey of Fountains. They had applied to St Bernard for counsel, and he received them into the Cistercian order, sending an experienced monk to instruct them. Thus, in one way or another, the Cistercians rapidly multiplied in England. Within thirty years fifty-one white monk abbeys existed in England and Wales, including the houses of the group of Savigny merged in 1147, and several of them had communities numbering hundreds. The Cistercian abbeys were almost always sited in remote valleys, on land that was uncultivated before their arrival and which has now once more returned to heath and waste, and it is difficult for the visitor of today to imagine the scene of teeming life that once existed around what are now often desolate heaps of stones or low mounds of grass. Visitors often ask whether the monks chose of set purpose the wild landscapes of Yorkshire and west Wales in preference to more homely and fertile sites. The answer is that they proclaimed their preference for 'undeveloped' sites, since manual work of all kinds was part of their vocation, and they were not allowed villein labour. Moreover, they desired the solitude of a wide unoccupied area, and it was natural therefore that benefactors should economise by giving away to the monks marginal or waste land. Often, indeed, the original site was so intractable either from a super-abundance of water or a lack of it, or from a soil that resisted all attempts at cultivation, that the monks removed themselves and all their gear to another site. It may be added, however, that buildings have often remained in these remote sites because there were no neighbours to covet the stones. Elsewhere, in Lincolnshire, East Anglia and Wiltshire, where population was greater and good building stone rarer, abbeys have vanished almost without a trace and the site has no visitors.

What, it may be asked, made the Cistercian call so compulsive in an England and France already covered with monasteries great and small? The basic answer is no doubt that the very rigour of the ideal, seen to be attained in practice by a contented and edifying family of men, was an incitement to an élite, and that the hard, energetic life appealed to some to whom the sedentary, cloistered, liturgical life of the black monks was repellent. And once a movement has begun well, whether it be of crusaders or boy scouts or supermarkets, there are always multitudes who will join in, usually to the great detriment of the original ideal. We must not imagine a Cistercian's life as boorish and bucolic, or even as inhuman and harsh. The first-hand account we have of it from a friend of abbot Ailred of Rievaulx shows us that great man discoursing with a group of young monks on all kinds of human, personal topics, and

Ailred, the 'Bernard of the north', is only one of a constellation of Cistercian writers, which includes William of St Thierry, who did not throw away their pen when they entered the Cistercian noviciate.

How is the gold become dim, and the fine colour changed! Within less than half-a-century of the first foundations in England the Cistercians were under a heavy barrage of criticism. They were ceasing to keep their statutes and owning serfs and churches; they were rich and grasping; they were harsh neighbours driving out the poor that they might have unbroken expanses for their ploughs and their sheep. The poor men of Cîteaux and Clairvaux, who had lived on grass and roots, were now wealthy landowners, whose flocks and harvests were an irresistible attraction for king John and his successors, perpetually out of cash. Gerald of Wales, one of the most vivid and fluent writers of the middle ages, nursed a feud with them and repeated *ad nauseam* the catalogue of Cistercians who had thwarted, tricked and opposed him.

The Cistercians were, as others before them had been, ruined by their own success. They had asked for only poor land, and poor land they had received. But the lay-brothers, who originated as an essential auxiliary, developed in numbers and skill so fast that, in the phrase beloved by their chroniclers, the waste howling wilderness bloomed and blossomed like the rose of Sharon. In other words hard work well directed helped to exploit the lands that were free of all manorial encumbrances and entanglements of partitioned and divided ownership. They could produce grain in bulk and use wide acres of wold and moor and down in some of the best wool-growing districts of England to build up a vast system of granges and collecting points where visiting merchants from Italy and the Low Countries could buy and load the annual wool clip. The most celebrated Cistercian churches and the beautiful halls and dormitories that remain, are a direct consequence of the sale of wool, which for four centuries at least held a place in the economy

This relief, a thirteenth-century wooden carving from the monastery of Pöhlde in Germany, shows a monk at his carpenter's bench.

similar to that held by coal in the nineteenth century.

But in early days they could draw generous hearts from afar. Here is Bernard, calling to two well-placed clerics of York, the one Henry Murdac, who heard the call and came – to become abbot of Fountains and archbishop of York – the other who turned away like the young man in the gospel:

He who has ears, let him hear the Lord calling aloud in the temple: 'He that thirsteth, let him come to me and drink: Come to me all ye who labour and are heavy laden, and I will refresh you'. Oh if thou mightest but once taste a little of that richness of the corn, with which Jerusalem is filled to plenty . . . How gladly would I give thee of that warm bread which, still steaming and drawn straight from the oven, Christ of his heavenly bounty so often breaks for his poor ones. Believe one who has experienced it. Thou wilt find among the woods something that thou didst never find in books. Stones and trees will teach thee a lesson thou didst never hear from masters in the school. Thinkest thou that honey cannot be drawn from the rock, and oil from the hardest stone? Do not the mountains drip with sweetness, and the hills flow with milk and honey, and the valleys abound with corn?[21]

And of one who had found the heavenly Jerusalem:

Yes; if you would know, it is Clairvaux. She is Jerusalem, joined to that which is in heaven with all the power of her mind; she imitates the life above, she shares it by spiritual kinship. This is his rest, as the Lord promised, for ever and ever; he has chosen it for himself as his dwelling; for there he finds, if not the vision, yet at least the expectation of true peace, even that peace of which it is written: the peace of God, which passeth all understanding.[22]

Another abbot could give the same message in a more direct form. Ailred is speaking in the person of a novice:

Our food is scanty, our garments rough; our drink is from the stream and our sleep often upon our book. Under our limbs there is but a hard mat; when sleep is sweetest we must rise at a bell's bidding . . . Everywhere peace, everywhere serenity, and a marvellous freedom from the tumult of the world. Such unity and concord is there among the brethren, that each thing seems

to belong to all, and all to each . . . To put all in brief, no perfection expressed in the words of the gospel or of the apostles, or in the writings of the fathers, or in the sayings of the monks of old, is wanting to our order and our way of life.[23]

In Ailred's writings we can see also, what we would not have expected, an eager group of young monks sitting around their abbot's cell:

In a group of brethren when I sat in their midst, and when all talked at once around me, and one asked a question, and another argued; and this one started problems from the scriptures, and another about conduct, another about faults and failings, and yet another about virtue, you alone were silent.[24]

And elsewhere Ailred's biographer tells of him equally occupied when painfully ill:

Coming to his cell and sitting there day by day, twenty or even thirty in number, his monks talked together, standing or sitting on the edge of his pallet on the floor, and talking with him as a child might talk with his mother.[25]

As happens with every successful concern, the Cistercians were soon paid the ambiguous compliment of imitation. The letters and decrees of Peter the Venerable show that Cluny was driven at least some distance in the direction of reform. Numerous monasteries, among them the whole congregation of houses based on Savigny in Maine, transferred themselves to Cîteaux. Others adopted some at least of the main Cistercian characteristics. New orders, such as the extremely numerous white canons of Prémontré and the English Gilbertines, borrowed heavily from the Cistercian statutes and uses. Even the military order of the Templars, when they applied to the pope for a rule of life, were passed on by him to Bernard. Above all, three prominent features of the Cistercian establishment became part of the common heritage of the church. The lay brotherhood answered so many problems that it was adopted at once by other new orders and passed, in various derivative forms, into innumerable institutes of men and women, and still exists, though under fire of criticism in our egalitarian age. The two disciplinary and administrative measures of annual general chapter and annual visitation were so clearly effective in the first century of Cistercian life that they were demanded by reformers as a panacea for the ills of traditional monachism, and were imposed upon all monks and regular canons by Innocent iii at the Fourth Council of the Lateran (1215).

Above all these particular influences, the Cistercians gave to the western church the first example of an integrated, universal (that is, supra-regional) religious order. Whereas the Cluniacs were a great army of monastic families, all members so far as words went of the one religious community of Cluny, but in fact subordinate houses bound by charter to follow the decrees of the abbot of Cluny and accept from him whomsoever he might appoint as their superior – in other words living as dependents of Cluny and under the monarchical rule of its abbot –, the Cistercians were a federation of equal autonomous houses, domestically independent and with an abbot who had an equal voice with all other abbots (including the abbot of Cîteaux) in framing decrees and passing judgments binding upon all. It is true that the Cistercian 'order' was an un-differentiated body of abbeys, with sovereign power residing in the totality of abbots in chapter. There were no 'provinces' and no 'abbot-general', and a monk could not be sent out of his own monastery save for serious disciplinary punishment. Moreover the 'order' itself stood by itself, it did not depend upon the papacy and was not based upon Rome any more closely than each independent black monk abbey. The fully articulated 'order', in which the individual belonged to the institute and not to one of its consti-tuent members, and which was directly placed at the disposal of the Roman curia, came only in the thirteenth century with the friars.

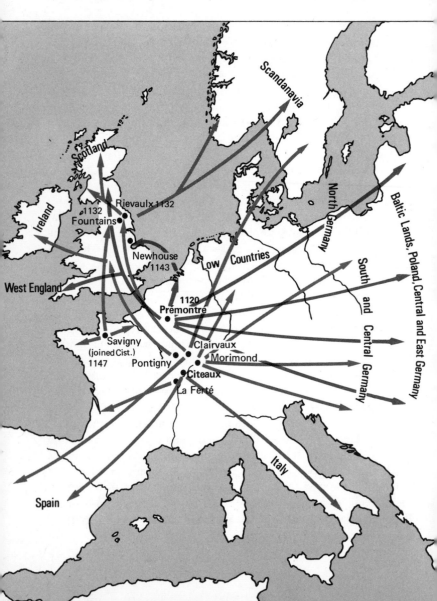

6 *Expansion of the Cistercians and Premonstratensians* The grey lines show the spread of the white monks with their principal areas of influence. Cîteaux founded chiefly in Italy and Spain; Clairvaux in France, Britain and Scandinavia; Morimond in the German empire; Savigny in west France and England. The purple lines show the expansion from Prémontré, largely confined to England and north and central Europe.

Nevertheless, the Cistercians, with their pregnant Charter of Love, were both a portent and an exemplar in a church that was rapidly becoming a centralised hierarchic body.

Finally, within the monastic order itself the Cistercians marked an epoch. Previous reforms and groups had arisen and existed within a single traditional framework. The Cistercians, perhaps at first unintentionally but later confessedly, stood forth as a body pledged to a reformed version of the Benedictine life different from all other reforms. They claimed explicitly to follow the rule literally; among themselves at first, and later openly, they claimed that theirs was the only true interpretation of that rule. Contemporaries may well have thought that either the white monks would eventually revert to type, as had so many previous reforms, or their interpretation of the rule would gradually win its way as the only standard. Neither of these possibilities became actual. The excellent statutes and constitution of the white monks, originally devised for a handful of houses, were successful both in holding together a vast organisation and in warding off all save integralist petitioners for union. Though the order, as we shall see, has had cycles of decline and decadence, it has never needed to revise in any great degree its intellectually logical and spiritually admirable programme as outlined and explained by Alberic, Stephen Harding, and Bernard. On the other hand, somewhat paradoxically, the monks who professed as a programme the integral observance of the rule of St Benedict have from their origin been known as Cistercians (or Bernardines) and regarded as a new twelfth century order, while the black monks, claiming with little historical accuracy and at least questionable justice to embody the spirit of St Benedict and the unbroken tradition of his teaching, who were nameless as a body in the twelfth century, assumed or were given in the fourteenth century the title of Benedictine, which common consent has allowed them to retain, and have in the course of time drawn into their loose federation almost all the 'reformed' congregations which have begun existence as separate 'orders'. Nevertheless the Cistercians may congratulate themselves as having found the only viable programme of reform in the history of Benedictine monachism, and they have been imitated in the past and in the modern world by black monk monasteries and congregations, while on the other hand attempts to outbid them such as those of Armand de Rancé and the revived Trappists have tended to return to the model of Cîteaux.

During the first half of the twelfth century the black monks had attained their highest point of numbers and houses, and by 1215 the Cistercians also had reached their fullness of flowering. It is true that, during the two centuries that followed, a considerable number of new foundations were made, but these were mainly in countries at the periphery of Europe, in Ireland, Scandinavia, Poland and Portugal, and even if the number of abbeys rose, the number of monks in many of the earlier foundations fell, so that the total number of white monks remained almost on a level, or even declined slightly, during the thirteenth century. At about the year 1200, then, monastic Europe had developed to its maximum. The face of the land was covered with monasteries of monks black and white, some great, some small, and in addition there were the quasi-monastic houses of the Premonstratensian canons and the less rigorous traditional or Augustinian ('Austin' or 'black') canons. Besides the abbeys there were numberless smaller establishments, conventual priories where the full round of liturgy was observed, priories of four or five monks, with less observance, and the 'notional' priories or cells, as they were called, which were often little more than administrative centres of one or more estates, often belonging to a distant, or in the case of Britain, to a continental or 'alien' abbey. Added together the estates of all these various houses of monks and canons, not including the estates of bishops and collegiate establishments, made up a very large fraction – perhaps as much as a quarter – of the exploited land of the country. Even a practised medievalist may be astonished to see the complete monastic map of any country of western Europe. In England and Wales alone, for which we have more complete information than for most other countries, the number of black monk houses had grown from fifty in 1066 to three hundred in 1200, while the white monks by 1200 had some seventy houses. Within those houses the number of black monks had risen during the same period from eight hundred to three thousand five hundred, while the white monks added some five hundred and fifty choir monks together with a larger number of lay-brothers. Such an extensive tenure of land by the 'dead hand' of undying corporations, and such numbers pledged to a life of fervour, were to pose problems for both church and society.

7 Monastic buildings

Any sizeable religious community needs certain apartments, a church, a place of assembly, a dormitory ('dorter' in medieval documents), a dining-hall (refectory or 'frater'), an infirmary ('farmery') and work-rooms, and place was found for all these in the early Egyptian Pachomian houses. In the eastern Mediterranean countries, however, these buildings did not at first form a single complex, but stood free, or in two or three groups, within an area surrounded by a wall, and this type of layout remained in eastern Europe and the Levant throughout the middle ages and into modern times.

In the west, many of the early monasteries were small. The indications that appear in both the rule of St Benedict and the rule of the Master suggest a single small straggling group of apartments, all on a single ground-floor level and without any conventional plan, in which the monks could pass in a few seconds from oratory to dormitory or refectory. The process of evolution from this small, irregular monastery to the formalised type that remained standard cannot be traced in detail, though it is certain that the process was complete in essentials by 800. It was conditioned by growth in numbers, but two features stood out from the rest and were universal: the large church and the quadrangular cloister. The large church was demanded not only by growing numbers, but more particularly by the growing solemnity and elaboration of ceremonies and chant and the multiplication of masses and processions.

The origin of the cloister, which became the distinguishing mark of a monastery in function, and which indeed gave its name to the establishment in many languages (e.g. chiostro, Kloster), is obscure. It is certainly a product of the Mediterranean region, probably of Italy, and it is probably derived, not as was at one time thought, from the *atrium* of the large Roman house, but from the court or *narthex* at the west end of Italian basilical churches,

The thirteenth-century night stairs in the south transept of the Augustinian priory of Hexham (Northumberland) are the most splendid and best-preserved example of this feature. By these stairs, the monks wearing 'night-shoes' descended from their dormitory at 2 a.m. going back there after office. During the day they used another stair debouching in the cloister.

such as may still be seen at Sant'Ambrogio at Milan. This was transferred in the monastery to form a quadrangle of which one corner filled the angle between the nave and transept of the church. The cloister had the great architectural advantage of providing a large open space round which the principal members of a complex could be grouped, and which gave to all these easy access and light. With the nave of the church forming one side, the dormitory and meeting-hall a second, the refectory and kitchens the third, and store-rooms and guest-rooms the fourth, the monastery was almost complete. Very early it was settled that the door to the outer world should be by the guest-rooms in the western range, while the infirmary was located away from the cloister and undisturbed, beyond the eastern range at the end furthest from the church. At first all was at ground level, but soon the dormitory was lifted to the first floor, with the assembly or chapter-room and novices' quarters beneath it, and a stairway giving direct access from the dormitory to the transept of the church became standard. Down

Top Moissac (Lot), an ancient Benedictine abbey on an important pilgrimage route to Compostela, became Cluniac in 1047. It is celebrated for its elaborate early Romanesque sculpture, of which the cloisters (1100) are the object of an unresolved controversy as to whether they precede Cluny and are therefore the primary source of Romanesque sculpture (E. Mâle), or whether priority should go to Cluny (K. Porter and K. Conant).

Bottom The ancient narthex or forecourt of the Basilica of Sant'Ambrogio at Milan (eighth to ninth century) is shown as a good example of the structure thought by many to have been the architectural forebear of the monastic cloister.

this the monks could pass rapidly for the night-choirs and return again without entering the cloister. Another stairway debouched into the cloister from the dormitory beyond the chapter-house. In Mediterranean countries the cloister was usually set north of the church, to provide a cool and shady walk where the monks could read and write. In northern countries, where sun and light are more desirable than shade, the cloister was normally sited south of the church, but local circumstances such as the presence of an earlier cemetery (as in England at Canterbury and Gloucester) or the needs of drainage and a water supply (as at Buildwas), or the slope of the land, might result in a northern position for the monastic buildings. The cloister, besides its function as a passage way, served as an area for study, writing and teaching. The walk alongside the church, the lightest and warmest in northern Europe, was reserved for the monks at work, and the book presses stood there against the wall of the church. For many centuries the arcading of the cloister was open to the air, but from the fourteenth century in northern Europe the openings were glazed, and in the fifteenth century it was common for studies (known as 'carrells') to be fitted against the windows between the pillars of the roof, with a bench and desk for the writer.

Beyond the cloister and church to the west lay the great court

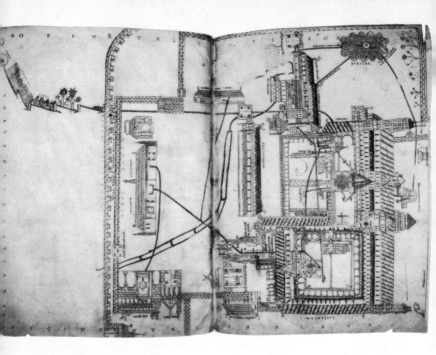

entered by the main gateway of the abbey and surrounded by
offices of all kinds, stables, bakehouse, brewhouse, grain stores, and
the offices of some of the monastic officials. Finally, a solid precinct wall pierced only by two or more gateways and posterns ran
round the whole site, enclosing church, monastery, courts, gardens,
orchards and graveyard. This may be seen still almost intact at
Canterbury Christ Church (the cathedral monastery), and traced
on air-photographs of many other sites.

Water and drainage were essential, even in the middle ages, for
any institutional complex of buildings. When a virgin site was
provided care was taken to choose the neighbourhood of a stream,
which was then canalised to flow through the precinct under the
buildings, especially the kitchens, infirmary and latrines, carrying
away refuse of all kinds. Great skill was shown in this, and where
at the present day dwelling houses have been set on monastic sites,
or parts of the monastic buildings adapted for modern use, under-
ground streams in strongly built stone tunnels can often be seen or

A twelfth-century plan for the water supply of Christ Church, Canterbury, cathedral priory. The cathedral is the Romanesque church of Lanfranc and his successors before the fire of 1174. The Benedictines were expert water engineers, surpassed only by the Cistercians. The water was fed to the buildings by gravity in stone conduits and lead piping.

heard in cellars and basements. For the purposes of drinking and washing, however, an entirely different source of water was used, usually obtained from a spring at some distance and conveyed by aqueduct or lead piping to one or more central cisterns, from which it was led off by the fall of gravity to taps or fountains in the cloister, kitchen, infirmary, sacristy and elsewhere.

The stereotyped order of buildings round the cloister was as follows. On the eastern range, prolonging the line of the south transept, lay the dormitory at first floor level, with the latrines (*necessarium*) continuing the range or at right angles to it in an eastward direction. At ground floor level between the south wall of the transept and the chapter-house was a 'slype' or narrow passage leading to the monks' graveyard, which usually lay to the east of the church. The chapter-room was placed near to the church to facilitate the move of the whole community each day after Prime, when they passed to the ceremonies of the daily chapter. The chapter-room was generally low, on account of the dormitory above, but sometimes it was entered from the cloister by an ante-room, which allowed the chapter-house to expand in height outside the range. Beyond this southwards lay the novices' quarters and the warming-room, where was the only fire outside the kitchen. Along the south walk lay the refectory, often like the halls of some colleges at Oxford and Cambridge, built over cellarage and approached by a wide flight of steps. This was usually, but not invariably, parallel to the walk of the cloister; occasionally it lay at right angles to it. West of the refectory lay the kitchens. The western range in black monk abbeys was chiefly devoted to cellarage, but when the abbot, who originally slept in the monastic dormitory, came to have quarters of his own, they were usually in the western range, along with some guest-rooms, and this in some monasteries developed into a complete 'house' for the abbot, with a large guest-hall attached. Two necessities of a modern monastery, a large working-room and a library were originally met, as has been noted, in the cloister, but accommodation was provided in winter in or near the warming-room, for those engaged in illumination and calligraphy, and in the fourteenth century many houses built libraries, often above the north walk of the cloister. A development also took place in the infirmary, which was originally a hall with an altar at the east end. Round this were constructed cubicles or cells for individual invalids, and often a small cloister and other accommodation were gradually added.

The main features of this layout had evolved by the beginning of the ninth century, as may be seen from the well known 'plan of St Gall', which may well represent a 'blueprint' circulated to abbeys at the moment of reform in 817, but it spread slowly. In England and elsewhere, monasteries had begun on a modest scale and on cramped or urban sites where the ideal plan was impracticable, and in any case few monasteries would have considered wholesale rebuilding for which there was no imperative practical necessity. Some monasteries however – Cluny is an instance – developed on 'classical' lines from the start, and this was so in particular with the eleventh-century abbeys of Normandy, whose planning influenced the many Norman monks who became abbots in England after the Conquest and rebuilt the old English abbeys on a larger scale. The Benedictines were individualists in this as in other respects, and the modern visitor must always be prepared for irregular siting. Thus at the cathedral monastery of Canterbury, the largest and one of the wealthiest houses, not only is the cloister to the north of the church, but the chapter-house, dormitory, prior's house and infirmary are all 'irregular' in site and plan. Indeed, almost all the abbeys at the heart of towns which they did not control were forced by their surroundings or by existing buildings to adapt themselves to the demands of the site, and for a black monk plan that keeps all the rules we must look for a site such as that of Bardney, which is neither in the midst of population nor hampered by earlier, irregular buildings. Glastonbury, though not without hindrances and peculiarities, comes near to adequacy as an example, as a result of recent excavations.

In contrast to the irregular, individualistic planning of the black monks, the Cistercian houses normally resemble each other with blueprint exactness. This is due to two circumstances. The first is the statutory authority of the Charter of Charity and other decrees, which demanded absolute uniformity of observance and practice in all houses descended from Cîteaux. Buildings were not specifically included in the list of objects concerned, but uniformity in plan was a natural corollary of spiritual and liturgical uniformity. The second circumstance, without which the decrees would have curtsied to material facts, was the free hand given to Cistercian planners and architects by the almost universal provision for the white monks of an open site far from habitation. Thus the builders were hindered only by a lack of funds or suitable materials from constructing an ideal monastery in a single operation, and in fact many abbeys in Europe were built, at least as regards their inner core, as a complete whole. The plan and design, and even the style of column, rib and moulding, would seem often to be based on a Burgundian pattern of which Fontenay, a daughter of Clairvaux constructed in Bernard's day, is an excellent example, if indeed it is not the type-abbey itself. In England the abbey that gives most clearly at the present day the full Cistercian plan is perhaps Kirkstall, and on the great majority of sites existing buildings, excavations, or air-photographs have revealed a striking uniformity. Naturally, some of the smaller and poorer houses began with simple, barnlike buildings, and the foundations or traces of these can often be seen alongside or beneath later works, while in a few cases – Kymmer in Merioneth, Wales, is one – the house never grew beyond its first shape. In continental Europe there are several examples of what Cistercian architects could do when intractable hillside sites were presented to them: Sénanque (Vaucluse) is a good example of this.

The Cistercian layout differed in several respects from that of the black monks, though a family resemblance persists throughout. Two demands, especially in early days, brought this about. The one was the Cistercian desire for seclusion and ritualistic simplicity. This made their churches, at least in the early decades, merely barns to provide space for the monks' choir and simple celebrations. Consequently, the Cistercian churches, in the heyday of the order's fervour, were without long architectural presbyteries or choirs, and without the large and elaborate shrines, Lady chapels, ambulatories and feretories of the cathedrals and pilgrimage churches. The second and more important circumstance was the presence of lay-brothers, religious persons but not clerics or choir monks, drawn largely from a different social level, occupied in garden and field and pastoral work, and reciting short and simple prayers. For them the plan provided what was in effect a second monastery with dormitory, refectory and infirmary separate from those of the monks. These were situated in the western range, where the Cistercians had no need for rooms for abbot and guests. The lay-brothers' dormitory, at first floor level, corresponded exactly with the monks' dorter in the eastern range. Below it was cellarage and, towards the southern end, the lay-brothers' refectory, served from the common kitchen, and their infirmary to the south-west of the western range corresponded to that of the monks to the south-east of the eastern range. The west walk of the cloister, or alternatively a passage within the range known as the 'lane' (French *ruelle*), gave them access to the western end of the church without disturbing the monks, and the western half of the nave was screened off to contain an altar and simple wooden forms at which the brothers could kneel.

The interior of an early Cistercian church thus differed from that of a black monk abbey. Whereas in the latter the greater part of the nave and aisles was open to visitors, while the eastern portion of the church was ultimately furnished with elaborately carved stalls, precious lecterns, candelabra, statues, screens and tombs, and the windows and screens glowed or gleamed with gold and bright colours, in the Cistercian church, wholly covered inside with whitewash, low screens divided monks from lay-brothers and ran behind the simple benches of the monks, and all was plain and colourless. Yet, as all who have seen a large and fairly intact Cistercian church are aware, the order grew to maturity at a moment of supreme architectural achievement in western Europe, and the simple arches, windows and pillars are of exquisite proportion and design. Even the domestic buildings, as at Fountains and many French abbeys, can be seen to have attained magnificence by reason of their extent and the purity of their style. In early days the abbot slept in the common dormitory and no guests were permitted in the monastic precinct, thus simplifying the complex of buildings. Later, even Cistercian abbots came to have a 'house' of their own, usually sited near the monastic infirmary, and a great Cistercian abbey such as Cîteaux or Clairvaux, with its offices, mills and stores, covered much ground. A feature was always the lay people's chapel near the great gate (*capella ad portas*).

8 Monastic summer and autumn

At the end of the twelfth century the monastic age, and in particular the Benedictine age of the church's history in the west, was drawing to a close. The great centuries of monastic literary and intellectual dominance were giving way to the age of the schools, with their logic, law and theology, that had sprung up and developed their organisation and which were offering intellectual interests and opening the way to ecclesiastical careers in which the monks could not keep pace with the masters of the growing universities. At the same time, the black monks were losing their recruits to the advantage of the grammar schools and the Cistercians, and were tending to draw their novices almost exclusively from the towns in which they were situated and from the estates which they owned. Even the Cistercians had begun to feel the effects of their reputation and their uncritical reception of novices. They were too numerous and too successful in material matters, and lost correspondingly in concentrated fervour. They had abandoned fairly generally the restrictions laid down by the Charter of Charity on the holding of serfs, churches, mills, tithes and the rest, and had become wealthy landowners and sheep farmers, though looking over Europe as a whole we can say that they held their high reputation throughout the thirteenth century. The strictures of Gerald of Wales, familiar to all medievalists and to many other readers, cannot be applied indiscriminately to the whole body of white monks.

Meanwhile the black monks throughout north-western Europe had gradually been caught in the web of social and political administration. In many of the larger abbeys the abbots had become vassals, tenants-in-chief, of the king, with the obligations of feudal service and attendance at the royal Council. They had set up establishments of their own which gave them a place apart from their community, and they spent a great part of the year either at court or in travelling from manor to manor. Even as early as 1170 and in the person of such a worthy man as Samson of St Edmundsbury, we can see the spiritual father lost behind the great magnate and skilful administrator, and we can note the distance between such a one and the earlier Anselm when abbot of Bec and the contemporary Ailred, the Cistercian of Rievaulx. As the abbeys grew in numbers and wealth, the administration became more complicated. Before the Conquest in England, all business relationships with the outside world had been conducted by the abbot and a single bursar or procurator, while the other officials such as sacrist, guestmaster and the like had concerned themselves solely with domestic matters. Now, gradually and from a number of causes, a general devolution of funds and duties had taken place and a group of officials, known as 'obedientiaries', ran their departments 'vertically' so to say, exploiting their own sources of revenue and collecting the produce of their lands, which they applied to the services and purchases of their department. Numbers of monks were thus fully engaged, and others partially, in managerial tasks, and what has been called the 'obedientiary system' was ubiquitous. These officials came to make up a class, which was distinguished from that of the 'monks of the cloister' who spent their time, apart from religious duties, in studying, copying manuscripts and illuminating them, seated in the cloister. Originally, and perhaps in some cases always, the imposition of an office was regarded as a burden, or at least as a toil, and the obedientiaries thought of themselves as bearing the burden and heat of the day as opposed to the sedentary cloisterers, but human nature must often have found relief from monotony in the activity and initiative that fell to the lot of the obedientiary, who could also claim considerable exemptions from church services and regular austerities. There can be little doubt that this system, which was to develop still more fully as estates grew in an expanding economy, helped to destroy the equality and simplicity of the common life which is one of the essentials of monasticism, and led also to the involvement of many in material interests and occupations which, as their lawgiver warned in his rule, were altogether disastrous for their spiritual life.

The last decades of the twelfth century were a time of stagnation in the history of the old monasticism, and they were marked both in England and elsewhere by a number of clashes between bishops and monks in which the former attempted to get control of monasteries in their dioceses, and the latter fought for complete independence of the ordinary. These contests were particularly numerous in England, where nine of the bishops had monks in their cathedral. As we have seen, this state of things had its origin in an epoch when almost all the bishops were monks, and when the monastic order was almost the sole reservoir and agency of religious and intellectual life in the Old English kingdom. By 1200 monastic bishops were rare, monks were no longer the mainspring of spiritual life in the land, but had become wealthy and powerful groups jealous of their rights. In consequence a kind of love-hate relationship prevailed. The monks pressed their claims against the bishop, but joined zealously with him in asserting the rights of his church and its lands. The bishop, for his part, resisted the partisan pressure of a community on his doorstep, but in many cases felt a personal friendliness towards a body of men who gave dignity and spiritual life to his cathedral, who lent aid in his lawsuits, and were on the balance no more quarrelsome than a chapter of secular careerists. In particular, the monks of Canterbury went through a half-century of mingled glory, controversy and misfortune. Their moral support of archbishop Thomas Becket might seem to have received its reward when the aftermath of his murder presented them with the shrine of the most celebrated martyr of Christendom, but tactless action on both sides led to a *cause célèbre* between the monks and two successive archbishops of Canterbury, Baldwin and Hubert Walter, over their respective rights and claims. No sooner had this dispute become quiescent than another flared up between the

Silos near Burgos in Castile, an ancient house reformed by Cluny in 1041, was suppressed in 1835–6 and revived early this century by monks of the Solesmes congregation exiled from Ligugé. The cloisters, built by the abbot, Santo Domingo (1041–73), are judged by Sacheverell Sitwell to have no equal in Castile from the Romanesque period.

monks and the king (supported by some bishops) over their claim to elect the archbishop, and this led to the exile of the greater part of the community. Similar, if less bitter, strife occurred at several other cathedral monasteries, but gradually a *modus vivendi* was established, and the communities of such houses as Canterbury and Durham remained to the end among the most active and observant in the land.

Meanwhile critics of the black monks were everywhere pointing to the success of the Cistercian institutions of visitation and general chapter in maintaining a high level of discipline, and at the Fourth Lateran Council of 1215 these and some other administrative reforms were imposed upon the independent houses of monks and canons. In every ecclesiastical province all houses were to meet in general chapter every fourth year under an elected president, with powers and duties similar to those of the white monks. They were also to maintain discipline. As the council also decreed the revival of the ancient custom of episcopal visitation, those houses that were not exempt from the bishop's control and depended directly upon Rome were visited by two authorities. Although the black monks looked askance at any system which restricted the freedom of the individual abbey, and resisted all endeavours to tighten the very loose bonds imposed by the council, in some countries, and particularly in England, the chapters repeatedly drew up and revised statutes for the whole body.

Almost immediately after the council, however, the prestige of the monks, both black and white, was threatened by the wholly unforeseeable emergence of the two first orders of friars. With these we are not directly concerned, but we may note that their early fervour, and their later capture of the palm of theology at Paris, Oxford and other universities, had the effect of diverting both spiritually and mentally gifted recruits from all the older orders. For this and other reasons the intake of the monks, which in the early twelfth century had come from all ranks of society, including the highest, and from sources distant from the monastery, now came predominantly from the burgess and free peasant class, and from the neighbourhood of the house.

Thus from the beginning of the thirteenth century onwards, in the west-central and western countries of Europe, the monks ceased to be the sole spiritual, intercessory, liturgical body in society, and came to be merely one of the numerous sections of the centralised church, along with the Roman curia, canons, friars, university theologicans and others. Indeed, their autonomy and their vast wealth in land now gave them the position, which they held for more than two centuries in regions and epochs of peace, of a social class with a foot in each of the two worlds of religious life and economic activity. With such a blend of monastic and adminis-trative activity they might still 'justify their existence' as a social class. In an economy which continued to expand until *c.* 1300 they found it more profitable to exploit their estates instead of leasing them out, and the careful and intelligent attention that they gave to all the problems of producing and marketing crops, enabled them to make full use of their varieties of arable and grazing land, and to bring marginal land under cultivation. The Cistercians had long practised as wool-growers; the black monks did not neglect sheep where, as in Kent or Somerset in England, conditions were favour-able, but cereals and legumes were the natural products of the manors on long-inhabited land, and such houses as Canterbury and Winchester were grain factories on a large scale.

Seen from another aspect, medieval monasticism in Europe became a static rather than a dynamic spiritual power from 1200 onwards. Dynamism passed to the friars and the lesser groups that imitated them. Such monastic reforms as occurred, principally in Italy, took the form of a more austere, solitary and simple life, without any constitutional or spiritual originality. Such were the

Silvestrines (*c.* 1247), the Celestines (1264), and the Olivetans (1344). Some of these became extinct, others formed small orders which still exist, mostly as congregations in the confederation of Benedictines; others again became canons or rejoined the stream of traditional monasticism.

The Cistercians did not maintain the *élan* and buoyancy they had shown during the lifetime of St Bernard, though in certain abbeys in every region, and in the peripheral provinces of Europe they showed for long examples of a holy life and an evangelical spirit. In the long run, however, wealth and the neglect of essential statutes brought mediocrity. The Cistercians enlarged their churches with apses and elaborate window tracery; their abbots, though never technically feudalised, built houses for themselves and became almost indistinguishable from Benedictines. Two major changes occurred among them. The first was a drift to the schools. This was begun under the English abbot of Cîteaux, Stephen of Lexington, who established a house, later St Bernard's College, at Paris. Successive popes warmly encouraged the move and Benedict XII imposed the obligation of sending one monk in every twenty to the university. Meanwhile the black monks had followed the fashion and had been served with the same obligation. Neither body in fact kept the letter of the law, for the full career of a master in law or theology was a long and expensive one, which also deprived a house in semi-permanence of its best minds, but the university monk became a familiar type. The rigid, formal course of studies, which never adapted itself to new needs or interests, was of little help in giving monks a permanent life-work at home, and perhaps the only gain was the competence in law and procedure which assisted those masters who became abbots. The other change among the white monks was the almost total disappearance of the lay-brother in regions of long-established cultivation. Several circumstances brought this about. One was the economic recession of the fourteenth century, which led many great landowners to turn back from high farming to the leasing of estates, thus removing the necessity for a large labour force. Another was the concomitant downward trend of population, intensified by the catastrophic pestilence of 1348–9. This both reduced the number of potential recruits and attracted many to the fields with the higher wages now available. Finally, many abbeys, especially those in wild regions, had always found an army of illiterate men difficult to handle in a life which was meaningless without a strong spiritual motive. In any case the lay-brothers disappeared almost entirely in many countries, and in consequence the Cistercian monastery came to resemble the black monk house, save for its rural situation and its smaller size.

If the early decades of the thirteenth century saw the flood tide of medieval monasticism hanging upon the ebb, this was in part because the life-blood of the church was filling new channels. Everywhere in the cities and populous countryside of north Italy, the Rhône valley and southern Germany the growing numbers of well-to-do artisans and townsmen were seeking a simpler, more evangelical and more communal religious life than the wealthy communities of monks and canons could offer. Several organised groups came into being, either to disappear or to be driven out of the church into heresy, and a crisis, not unlike that of the fifteenth century, seemed to threaten a general collapse or revolt. The situation was saved by the simultaneous appearance of two saintly leaders of genius, the one, Francis of Assisi, calling all who would hear him to a brotherhood of absolute poverty in the service of Christ, the other, Dominic the Spaniard, harnessing the same desire for poverty and service to the work of preaching the faith to heretics and heathens. Between them they created a new kind of devotee, the friar, whose aim was not solitude or seclusion from the world, and whose occupation was not primarily liturgical worship,

uturū,ut Chriſtus contēptis
,ſuū illud ſit exacturus præ
npe charitatis. Alius oſtenta
lū,omni piſcium genere di
lius pſalmoꝛ centum effun/
. Alius ieiuniorū myriadas
,& toties unico prandio pe
imputabit aluum. Alius tan
niaꝛ aceruū proferet,quan
tem onerarijs nauibus uehi
s gloriabit ſexaginta annos
tam pecuniā,niſi digitis du/

uidem⁹ex his tot diſ
criminib⁹,magnasac
periculoſasnaſci diſ
cordias. De quibus
qd attinet multa di
cere,cum nemo neſci
at꞉ Suū illud ſit exa
cturus.) Nam Chri/
ſtus in illa orōne ple
na feruoris & charita
tis. quam ultimā cū
ſuis diſcipulis habu/
it,poſt multam chari
tatis cōmendatiōem
ita demum præcepit,
αὐτῆ ὅϛιν ἡ ἐντολὰ ἡ
ἐμὴ,ἵνα ἀγαπῆτε ἀλλὴ

but who went up and down the ways of men calling them to the
following of Christ and preaching to them Christian doctrine. Each
of the two great bodies influenced the other while retaining its own
spirit. Both became vast centralised organisations under a single
head and governing body, both stood for poverty and dependence
on alms rather than on fixed material sources of income, and both
reached a position of eminence in the great flowering of philosophy
and theology in the universities of Europe, particularly Paris and
Oxford. For more than a century they attracted a majority of the
most earnest and brilliant of successive generations of youth
throughout Europe and became the preachers, confessors, spiritual
directors and theological masters of their age. The two first orders,
the Friars Minor. (the Lesser Brethren) of Francis and the Friars
Preachers of Dominic, dissimilar twins over whose birth and
infancy pope Innocent III had watched, were to exercise mutual
influence upon each other and were found together all over Europe
as daily rivals who would join as allies against attack. The Franciscans were from the beginning the more numerous, but were riven
by a succession of acrid controversies over the observance of their
Founder's conception and command of Christlike poverty. After

more than one schism within the order, and the final departure of the intransigent rigorists into heresy, a reforming group known as Observants became independent in the fifteenth century, and a third group, the Capuchins, appeared in the age of the Reformation. The Dominicans, a smaller but more united body, had in St Thomas Aquinas (1226–74) the greatest thinker and theologian of the age, the 'master of all' (*doctor communis*), but his system and his supremacy were challenged by the Franciscan John Duns Scotus (1266–1308), and it was over two centuries before Aquinas was universally accepted as a norm of orthodoxy. The two other major orders, the Carmelites and the Austin Hermits, began as scattered eremitical bodies, which united, the former spontaneously, the latter under papal pressure, and accepted an organisation and programme similar to that of the Dominicans. The friars of all orders established themselves in cities, university towns and the larger market-towns throughout Europe. Protected and privileged by successive popes, they worked, now in concurrence, now in competition with the parochial clergy, providing preachers, confessors and spiritual directors who for at least two centuries surpassed all other members of the clergy in spiritual energy, doctrinal knowledge and pastoral ability. They long maintained their hold upon the esteem of the poor, and of the urban populations, but from the mid-fourteenth century onwards their implication in purely social and secular interests, and their avidity for alms and benefactions of all kinds, to say nothing of the lowering of moral standards and their tiresome ubiquity, helped to make them objects of criticism and satire, and later the scape-goats of the whole clerical establishment at the hands of hostile unbelievers and reformers. Chaucer's monk and friar, though figures of the human comedy touched with the poet's satire, are fair presentations of the contemporary image – the monk worldly and self-indulgent, but socially respectable, the friar importunate, loose in morals, seeking money by flattery, and humouring the minor superstitions of his world. The monks who were the target of the sharpest arrows of Erasmus and his followers were not for the most part members in the monastic orders, but friars who were the principal purveyors of the 'mechanical' religion of fasting, penances, indulgences and multiple prayers that seemed to the reformers to have replaced the simple Christian virtues and services of the old age.

The centuries between 1200 and 1500 saw a gradual decline in the external maintenance of the spiritual ideals of monasticism. This can be seen by a glance at the decrease of austerity, the abandonment of the fully common life, and the breakdown of the spiritual relationship between abbot and monks.

While fasting and abstinence are no infallible test of holiness of life, and though the rule of St Benedict was remarkably moderate in its day with its dietary demands, history and all spiritual experience suggests that a monastery, by and large, may be roughly gauged by its diet. In this matter in the middle ages the touchstone was the eating of meat. The rule states categorically that fleshmeat may be eaten only by invalids, and it is clear that as late as the eleventh century this abstinence was maintained in all normally observant houses. Meat was allowed only in the infirmary and at the abbot's table when he ate with guests. From the end of the twelfth century at latest the rule was breached more and more widely. Two loopholes were found. The one was the abbot's table. When the abbot invited monks to dine with him and his guests they could eat meat, and gradually the custom grew up by which the abbot followed a rota of invitations to his table for all members of the community, whether guests were there or not. A second loophole was the infirmary. The custom of periodic blood-letting, which seems to have come in after the age of Charlemagne, to disappear shortly before 1400, gave occasion for a visit to the infirmary followed by a day or two of recuperation during which meat might lawfully be eaten. Later, in the early fourteenth century, permission was given for all to take meat on three or four days of the week, and this was canonically established by Benedict XII in 1336. To preserve appearances, however, meat was never served in the main refectory, but in another dining-room which the community attended by relays.

Quite apart from the matter of meat, the spirit of the rule was throughout the middle ages transgressed in many houses by the provision of rich and abundant fare, especially on feast days. A *locus classicus* for this occurs in the *Apology* of St Bernard, where he has Cluny in mind; and it was a subject upon which Gerald of Wales never tired of expatiating.

The full common life was for monks following the rule the true way of observing spiritual and material poverty. It implied, or was meant to imply, absolute absence of private ownership. This was in the main faithfully practised until the fourteenth century, when it broke down in two principal ways. It became common for obedientiaries to have quarters of their own outside the cloister in which they did business, slept, ate, and even entertained members of the community or externs. Secondly, it became the custom to issue small sums to each member of the community which they could use for purchasing clothes, books and small personal comforts, in addition to gifts to relatives and private almsgiving. This was known under the blanket term of 'spice money' or 'wages'. It was a fixed amount, differing from monastery to monastery, and increased by a bonus on the occasion of private celebrations, such as a priest's first mass, and this, together with other amenities, such as the provision of wainscotted compartments in dormitory and cloister, tended to change the monastic life into that of a college.

Finally the mutual and intimate relationship between abbot and monk, always and in every age peculiarly important and peculiarly vulnerable, deteriorated steadily during this period. The abbot, entangled in political, feudal and social engagements, left the cloister for an establishment of his own which grew steadily in size and comfort. Worse still, he was often away on business of the king or of his house, and even when no public business called him away, he spent the greater part of the year on one or other of his manors. It became, indeed, common, almost customary, for the abbot to spend even the time when he was 'at home' not in the monastery but in a manor house a mile or two away, where the monks could visit him. Thus gradually from the abbot of the rule, who existed solely to rule and guide his monks, he became a distant authority, scarcely known to the monks of the cloister and approached only when some personal or administrative problem demanded counsel or decision, until at last he became simply a kind of patron or employer – 'my master', as the English monks of early Tudor days referred to him. We can follow the change by looking at the lives of Anselm at Bec, Suger at St Denis, Samson at Bury, Thomas de la Mare at St Albans, and Prior More at Worcester.

So it was when things were at their best, and the abbot was a monk of the house elected by his brethren and nominally in residence. Such was the case in the British Isles. But on the continent, and particularly in the Latin Europe of Italy, France and Spain conditions were far worse. There the plague of *commendam* blighted monastic life both in flower and fruit. An office given *in commendam* was bestowed on someone who was not the lawful and canonical possessor in order that he might protect the interests of the benefice or institute until such time as a lawful owner might be appointed or restored. Gradually it came to be used by popes as a means of maintaining or rewarding those who had served them or had suffered the loss of their rightful office. As time went on and the papacy felt the financial and political strains of residence at Avignon (1309–77) and the subsequent Great Schism (1378–1417), the popes – both of them, when there were two – used *commendam* on a vast scale to maintain curial officials and to make allies abroad. The right was transferred to monarchs and the conditions of bestowal and qualifications of the grantee became less and less stringent. Cardinals, bishops, kings, magnates became titular abbots, and some houses might see neither lawful abbot nor commendatory for decades on end, while at others the lay holder of the abbacy might be only too visible as an expensive and rapacious resident on the nearest abbatial manor. In theory the commendatory existed to administer and protect the assets of the house. In fact the most conscientious might content themselves with leaving the agreed portion of the funds for the convent's use, or at least giving a fair pension to the monks, while themselves taking the abbot's portion for their own benefit, but an unscrupulous man could impoverish and dilapidate a monastery, scamp repairs, fell timber, bully the monks and leave the place in every way worse off than he found it. Human nature can be astonishingly resilient and adaptable, and with a good prior a disciplined community might seem to fare none the worse, but taken on average the results were lamentable. At the very best the monks were deprived of the power of directing their own development and of having at their head one who could lead them or join with others in counsel and reform. A benevolent commendatory and a good prior might be better than a bad abbot, but such a line of argument would not lead far. In actual fact, the commendatory system was a scourge, petrifying minor abuses and sapping the spiritual and material strength of a house. It may be seen at its worst in Scotland at the end of the fifteenth century and in France during the seventeenth.

Only a little less harmful was the practice of provision as applied to abbeys of certain categories by the papacy, or permitted by Rome to monarchs. This deprived the monks of their right of election and put in a stranger who might have neither the desire nor the ability to rule a monastery on spiritual lines.

Besides these particular misfortunes and malpractices, the monasteries of the later middle ages, in common with the whole body politic of the church, deteriorated, as any great class or institute must deteriorate, when it is no longer an organic part of a changing society. Monasticism had expanded too widely, and had been too richly endowed, in a particular phase of religious enthusiasm. It had now been outbidden by new orders and associations, and had lost its monopoly of culture and economic skill. Among its invisible losses had been that of a universal employment peculiarly suited to its way of life, that of copying and embellishing manuscripts of all kinds. In this, competition from the paid professional, who could work longer hours and meet the demands of wider markets, had made itself felt from about 1200 onwards, and competition became annihilation when printing began to supplant writing. Under medieval conditions it was impossible for monks to re-enter the world of education, and the Reformation came before scholarship and its appurtenances offered a career possible for religious to follow. The cry that monks were idle cloisterers, often raised in the late middle ages, was comprehensible then as it would not have been in the Norman monasticism of the eleventh century.

A single monastic body, small in numbers but significant in the quality of its members, escaped almost all the ills that have been retailed in the foregoing pages. The Carthusians, half hermits, half community monks, had grown slowly in France and at the end of the twelfth century had adopted the constitution of an order, with annual general chapter, regular visitations, and the presidency of the prior of the Grande Chartreuse. Their customs had been excellently stereotyped by prior Guigo I, prior 1110–36, and from the first a rigid discipline had governed their imposition upon all foundations, and controlled the training and admission of recruits. The order, alone among the monastic bodies of Europe, has remained to the present day almost unchanged in observance, never reformed and never needing reform, relatively small, but with a spiritual influence disproportionate to its numerical strength. Paradoxically at first sight, the strict Carthusians prospered and increased when all others declined, and the two centuries 1350–1550 were the epoch of their widest dispersion and influence – indeed the only period in which their mark on the external life of the church, by their writings and their reforming zeal, has been at all notable. Previously concentrated in French-speaking lands, they spread to the Low Countries, Rhineland and Italy, and the small group in England trebled its numbers. This may have been in part a reaction of fervent spirits against the general decline, and a reflection in the regular life of the wave of mystical experience which characterised the fourteenth century. From another point of view, the readiness of monarchs and magnates to found or to support Charterhouses came partly from the prevailing eagerness to establish reliable centres of intercessory prayer for a dynasty or a family. The Carthusians made themselves more familiar to the world in this century by accepting, perhaps even desiring, urban rather than desert sites, and the presence of such men at the very heart of cities such as Paris, Cologne, London and others made them a cynosure and a centre of spiritual direction.

9 Byzantine monasticism

We saw on a previous page how rapidly monasticism spread in all the lands round the eastern Mediterranean. Southwards and eastwards of Antioch the monks were mostly of the hermit or the semi-hermit (*lavra*) type, save for such Pachomian monasteries as survived in Egypt. All this territory was overrun by Islam in the early decades of the seventh century, and the monastic life that survived continued without change of character, but it had little influence upon the rest of Christendom and received no new impulses or ideas from Byzantium or the west.

In Asia Minor, on the other hand, the monasticism that spread was of the Basilian kind, that is, one with a moderate but fully regulated degree of community life, and it was this that became preponderant in the Byzantine empire, though hermits and extreme ascetics of the pillar-saint type were not unknown. The monastic life was slow to reach Constantinople, but once there it increased steadily; by the time of Justinian, in the sixth century, there were some eighty monasteries in the capital or on the shores of the Bosphorus and Propontis, almost all of moderate size. From early days Byzantine monachism developed on lines quite different from the west, though there were inevitably resemblances, some of them striking as evidence of the basic Christian tradition. In both east and west the monks as a body were very wealthy, with wide estates and certain fiscal privileges. But in the west there was no parallel to the great cities of the east, least of all to Constantinople, while the east had no small cathedral cities and towns dominated by a monastery as its religious and economic centre. Nor were there in the east the conditions of fragmented jurisdiction and feudal devolution that made of the abbots of western Europe territorial magnates and figures in political and social life. In the eastern empire the cities, and especially Constantinople, contained a large proportion of the monastic population of the land.

As a consequence, the parts played by monks in eastern and

A page from the *Studion Psalter*,
written and illustrated *circa* 1066
by Theodore of Caesarea, of
the monastery of Studion,
Constantinople.

125

western society were different. While in the west, at least before
c. 1150, the monks had a near monopoly of spiritual and intellectual
leadership, and an economic and social position of great strength,
while remaining apart from the daily lives and interests of the
baronage and the townsfolk, in the east monks from various
monasteries met and mingled in the cities and took a leading part
in the theological discussions, the political upheavals and the current
problems of ethics and piety. Questions such as the morality of an
emperor's marriage or remarriage, and deeper issues such as the
veneration of images, were debated and sometimes even decided by
the monks of the capital, while at certain epochs they had a name
for rioting and violent action. On occasion, they gathered in
groups or mobs, acting quite literally as 'pressure-groups'. In a
highly civilised and differentiated society it was neither necessary
nor possible for monks to lead movements of thought or literature,
but on the other hand, as confessors and spiritual directors and
writers, and as individual holy men, they had a position in the
devout life of the country without parallel in the medieval west,
though not unlike that taken up by the Jesuits, Capuchins and other
religious in seventeenth-century France. Moreover, in the realm of
art they had as high a position as miniaturists and painters as had
the monks of the west in the eleventh and twelfth centuries.

Their status was regulated by the early councils in decrees which
passed also into western canon law, and in the sixth century the
emperor Justinian laid down a body of legislation that remained in
force till the end of the empire. This, and the differing social
conditions, together with the Byzantine reverence for a tradition
which had never been broken, preserved eastern monachism as a
whole from complete secularisation and from the rhythm of
decadence and reform experienced by the west, as it also stood in
the way of the formation of new orders and the diversification of
vocations. By and large, especially after the Muslim conquests, the

Byzantine empire was a culturally and spiritually homogeneous society, of which the monks were a section, not a tier. Byzantium, unlike western Europe, remained to the end a religious corporation. Emperor, monks, bishops, priests and people, whatever factions or palace revolutions might take place, remained conscious of their common bond and mutual interdependence in religious matters in a way not possible in the widely spread, nationally divided, strongly hieratic Christendom of the west.

In their daily life, as also in many features of their organisation, the Byzantine monks were close cousins of the black monks of the west. The round of offices, the daily horarium, the ceremonies and discipline, even the spiritual doctrine were in essence identical. A symbiosis, if not a union, of the two was at certain times not only conceivable but actually existent. There were Greek monks in or near Rome at more than one juncture, and there were Latin monks on Mount Athos. Nevertheless, the major differences remained. In the east the monks remained essentially unchanged during the western 'middle ages'. Before the ninth century they did not act as missionaries or colonists as did the Irish and Anglo-Saxon and other western monks, and while they often supported financially, they did not themselves operate educational, hospital or other eleemosynary undertakings. They did not undertake priestly pastoral work, either on parishes or from their monastery; on the other hand, owing to the firm custom of appointing only celibates to the episcopate, the majority of eastern bishops were taken from the monasteries.

Early monasticism at Constantinople produced certain families or types peculiar to the east. One such were the so-called 'sleepless' monks of a large monastery founded by Alexander of Chalcis, and finally settled at Constantinople. Here a large community, divided into three choirs, kept up a ceaseless chant of psalms, hymns and prayers in relay throughout the day and night. Another was the

celebrated monastery founded by the consul Studius in 463 and governed centuries later by St Theodore (abbot 798–826) who gave to the large community, said to have been one thousand strong, a strict way of life and an elaborate scheme of organisation, which was adopted by other houses and served to keep observance and discipline at a high level. The Studites remained for long the élite of the monastic body, with a great influence which even emperors neglected at their peril. Theodore was a man of great wisdom, with a genius for organisation, and his monastery had a character not unlike that of Bec in the days of Lanfranc and Anselm. His writings and regulations continued for centuries to inspire and to inform, giving precision and completeness to the teaching of St Basil in some such way as Benedict in the west crystallised the doctrine of the fathers of the desert as set out by Cassian. But neither Basil nor Theodore ever became for the eastern monks what the rule of Benedict or the Charter of Charity became in the west. Byzantine monasteries had no rule. They followed a general scheme common to all, derived ultimately from the Pachomian

Left A monastery on Mount Athos.
Right Meteora (Thessaly).

rule and the instructions of St Basil, as modified by conciliar and imperial legislation and amplified by later liturgical practice. In addition, each monastery on foundation received a charter (*typicon*) regulating the daily life and liturgical observances. This corresponded in general to the 'uses' or 'customaries' of western monasteries, but whereas the latter could be carried from one monastery to another and applied within the framework of the Benedictine rule to a whole group (e.g., that of Cluny), the *typicon* was drawn up for a single house and included matters which in the west formed part of the rule.

Great and permanent as was the influence of the monastery of Studius with the teaching of Theodore, a still more influential and permanent focus of the monastic life came into being more than a century later (963–4) with the foundation of the great *lavra* on Mt Athos by St Athanasius at the suggestion of the emperor Nicephorus II Phocas. Athos, a narrow and mountainous peninsula some forty miles long, stretching out into the Aegean sea from near Salonica, and chosen originally for its inaccessible solitude, soon

130

The Monastery of the Caves at Kiev, the most famous of early Russian monasteries, was founded by a hermit Antony, in a cave above the river Dnieper *circa* 1050. Twenty years later abbot Theodore moved the brethren into a monastery above ground, of which the illustration shows the later gateway.

became a kind of monastic republic with monasteries of all kinds clinging to the faces of the cliffs like nests of house-martins. The Byzantine nucleus was soon joined by foundations from the newly formed European empire of the Greeks. Serbia, Rumania, Bulgaria and Russia contributed and endowed monasteries. Besides some twenty large establishments there were ultimately some two hundred small houses and more than four hundred hermitages. The whole complex was self-supporting, both from gardens, orchards and vineyards on Athos and estates on the mainland given by bene-factors, and it formed a colony which in its heyday was unique in Europe and perhaps in the world. Pilgrims and visitors came in large numbers, and added to the funds, the artistic treasures and the precious manuscripts. As is well known, no woman nor female animal of any description was (or is) allowed to set foot on Athos. In later centuries similar groups of monasteries, plastered on cliffs or perched on crags and hill-tops, came into being at Meteora in Thessaly and Mistra near the site of ancient Sparta in the Peloponnese. These, and some houses on Athos, were literally inaccessible on foot and were reached only by a rope and basket, or by a primitive form of crane.

When Byzantium extended her influence, part missionary and part political, over the Slav nations of Europe monasticism was part of the Christian inheritance of the converts. In Bulgaria monasteries were founded by the tsar Peter in the tenth century, and others in Serbia by the royal house. In Russia the first monas-tery was the creation of Yaroslav, son of Vladimir, prince of Kiev, probably soon after 1015. This, and other early Russian houses, was similar to the imperial and aristocratic foundations of Con-stantinople. The most celebrated and influential monastery of early Russia was, however, the Monastery of the Caves at Kiev. This owed its existence to a Russian monk at Mt Athos, Anthony, who returned to his native land *c*. 1050 and dwelt in a cave in the hillside

above the river Dnieper. Disciples gathered round him and a large cave was dug for them; the monastic teaching and loyalty there derived directly from Athos and the Monastery of the Caves looked back thither as to its spiritual home. A change came when Theodosius, abbot from 1062 to 1074, removed the brethren from the caves to a house above ground, and obtained from Constantinople a copy of the Studite rule. This was introduced and transformed the Monastery of the Caves into a house with a fully common life. Theodosius is seen in the *Life* written by Nestor, one of his monks, as a man of firm, but gentle and moderate character, with a certain resemblance to Benedict of Nursia. His monastery remained until the Mongol invasions as the very heart of Russian monachism, and the nursing mother of innumerable bishops. One of these, Vladimir, a bishop in north-eastern Russia, wrote to a monk of his old house:

I tell you truly, I would immediately set at naught all this honour and glory, if only I could be one of the stakes in the fence standing beyond the monastery gates, or if I could lie as a bit of dirt in the Monastery of the Caves, so that men would trample upon me, or if I could become one of the poor, begging by the gates of the monastery.[26]

This house, like some of its contemporaries in the west, was a cradle of the national historical literature in the form of chronicle writings.

The Mongol invasions of the thirteenth century destroyed most of the monasteries, which were for the most part in urban or suburban localities. The monasteries of later Russian history were by contrast in remote sites in forests and many in distant parts of northern Russia.

Byzantine monachism also had changed in spiritual outlook by this time. There had been a revival of both spiritual and cultural life in the monasteries from the eleventh century onwards, inspired by the personality and writings of St Symeon (949–1022) an abbot in Constantinople and perhaps the greatest medieval mystic of the eastern church. Byzantine mystical theology, like that of the west, had its roots partly in the direct evangelical teaching of the fathers of the desert, which was schematised by Evagrius of Pontus, who laid excessive emphasis on the constant exercise of concentrated recollection and the attainment of absolute 'apathy'. In addition, as in the west, there was the influence of Neoplatonism as Christianised by (the pseudo) Denis the Areopagite. In the later Greek empire true evangelical mysticism was obscured by theologians who attempted to express all experience in terms of dogma, law and logic, and enthusiasts and spiritual directors who taught that the mystical experience could be obtained by merely human efforts, whether in silencing the faculties or in some 'open sesame' of continual prayer or mental effort. In Byzantine monachism, the controversy, which has many similarities with the later Quietist and anti-mystical controversy in the French church, concerned the school of spirituality known as hesychasm (from the Greek word *hesychos* signifying calm, quiet). The revival of interest in mystical prayer – which was by coincidence almost exactly contemporary with the Neoplatonist mysticism of Eckhart in the Rhineland – drew inspiration from the traditional and orthodox spirituality of Symeon, but taught a quasi-physical technique of a fixed gaze, regulated breathing and the repetition of the 'Jesus prayer' as a means of attaining receptive, contemplative silence. This was attacked (1341) by a monk Barlaam, originally from a monastery in Calabria, who proposed to teach mystical knowledge by dialectic. He was countered by a hesychast monk and theologian, Gregory Palamas, but the latter's teaching on the mystic's vision of God was in turn denounced as unorthodox, as bringing the unknowable God within the range of human (though admittedly God-aided) cognition. The theological controversy that ensued was technical and complicated, with a considerable resemblance to that between Bossuet and Fénelon three centuries later, and as in the French dispute, neither side had a monopoly of orthodoxy or good sense. On the whole Palamas stood out as the more influential, and a modified form of hesychasm, resembling the contemplative prayer of western spiritual writers, prevailed in practice, especially in the Russian monasteries of a later age.

The cenobitic regime, though by far the most common, was not the only form of organised monastic life in the Byzantine empire. In the last centuries of Byzantium the so-called idiorhythmic (*idios*=private, personal; *rhythmos*=routine, order of life) system came in, particularly on Mt Athos. In this monks lived in small families, each with its own 'provost', within the monastery. Private ownership was allowed on the personal level, while the monastic funds supplied overhead expenses. The various groups rarely met together socially, but in some cases they performed the eucharistic liturgy and the divine office in common. On the economic level, there is some similarity between this arrangement and the groups or 'messes' and 'wage-system' found in some western monasteries, and many nunneries, in the fifteenth century, but whereas the latter was simply a breakdown of community life, the idiorhythmic regime had, at least in origin, a firm spiritual and disciplinary basis. As we shall see, it spread later to Russian monasteries.

10 Late medieval reforms

The conciliar epoch of the early fifteenth century, familiar to readers of history for its cries for a reform which it failed to bring about, was not wholly without fruit in the realm of monastic history. The Council of Constance (1414–18) has until very recently been considered by historians solely as an exercise and a clash of the 'conciliar' and 'anti-conciliar' parties. It had however as its prime object a general reform of the church, and among those present in early days were Benedictine abbots in large numbers, from the Italian peninsula, from France, from Germany and even from England. In 1417 a synod of monks, sponsored by the council, met at Peterhausen near Constance. After long deliberation the fathers produced a reiteration of the reforming statutes of Benedict XII, and appointed visitors to apply these in German-speaking lands.

A result of this was a revival of the long-lapsed provincial chapters in Germany and Austria, and the crystallisation of several attempts of reform. One of these had begun at Kastl in Bavaria, where the strict Cluniac customs of the eleventh century had been revived. The meetings at Constance and Peterhausen led to the reform of a group of Bavarian abbeys along the lines of Kastl. It might well have developed, had it not been overtaken by two other movements which had a more powerful appeal and greater support. The first of these, known as the reform of Melk, took its rise from a desire of Albert V of Austria to found a fervent abbey. A handful of German monks, then at the ancient abbey of Subiaco which had recently been reformed from Sta Giustina of Padua, were summoned by the council and despatched to Melk, an abbey now well known to tourists from its magnificent site on a hill above the Danube, but then on the point of extinction. The venture (1419) prospered, and from Melk abbeys far and wide in Austria and Bavaria were reformed, among them such famous houses as Kremsmünster, Hirsau and Fulda. The union of Melk was based upon the customs of Subiaco, that is, the rule of St Benedict strictly observed, and lay-brothers were introduced. Neither Melk nor Kasti formed congregations in the canonical sense; they were free unions, and as such liable to dissolve.

More permanent success attended a third venture, that of Bursfeld, during the council of Basle (1431–7). Bursfeld, an abbey in Hannover, then in a state of decadence, received as abbot from the Duke of Brunswick in 1433 a distinguished reformer, John Dederoth. He, assisted by John Rode, abbot of St Martin's at Trier, laid the foundations of the congregation of Bursfeld, which was given juridical status by the council of Basle. Bursfeld stood in many ways to the reform of Sta Giustina, to which we shall soon turn, as Hirsau, four centuries earlier, had stood to Cluny. While insisting on similar observance it held fast to the traditional autonomy allowed to every house. The annual chapter-general was composed of all the abbots and priors actually ruling monasteries. The abbot of Bursfeld was its perpetual president, but at his election the domestic community was afforced by various officials of the whole union. Between chapters the abbot of Bursfeld was visitor-general and had abbatial rights over all in controversial matters, but the individual abbots had full power over all the spiritual and temporal affairs within their own monasteries. The reform of Bursfeld was directed against prevalent decadence and its observance was austere. The union increased its membership for two centuries, and weathered the Reformation, expiring only in 1802. In the early sixteenth century an attempt was made to merge the three German-speaking groups mentioned above; it failed, largely through the unwillingness of the others to accept the severity of Bursfeld. All these bodies, and in particular Melk and Bursfeld, encouraged intellectual pursuits and sent their promising students to the university. Their spiritual and scholarly writing was of a high order, and historians of monasticism in Germany owe much to Trithemius, abbot of Spanheim.

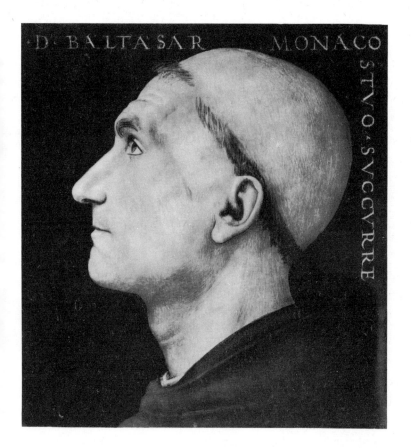

·D· BALTASAR MONACO STVO·SVCCVRRE

These reforms had been wholly traditional. A more original and more influential attempt to meet the evils of the times came from Italy. In 1408 Pope Gregory XII, a pontiff of the 'Roman' line who abdicated in the cause of unity, appointed a zealous Venetian patrician, Ludovico Barbo, commendatory abbot of the collapsed Cluniac abbey of Sta Giustina at Padua. Barbo took the habit as an authentic monk and reformed the abbey; novices came in numbers and a small congregation was formed. At first the abbot of Sta Giustina was the supreme authority, but this was resented by the daughter houses. Finally Eugenius IV, a Venetian and a friend of Barbo, gave the group a completely novel constitution in which

the congregation, not the individual abbey, was the unit to which all made profession, and the supreme authority was the annual general chapter which, through a small committee of definitors, appointed short-term abbots (eligible for election elsewhere on the same conditions) and visitors who had complete authority between chapters. These were only the main provisions of a detailed way of life which, speaking loosely, added to the skeleton machinery of the existing Benedictine congregation the governing body of a religious order such as the Dominicans, while reducing the monarchical abbot to the level of an annual superior. It had, however, the supreme merit of leaving no foothold for a commendatory abbot, or indeed of an abbot living apart from his monks. Nor was the machinery of government the only novelty. Barbo and his successors were 'modern' also in their conception of the spiritual and intellectual life of their monks. They took from the Rhineland mystics and the Brethren of the Common Life in the Low Countries their emphasis on systematic private meditation and prayer, and from the humanists in Italy the practice of scholarship as an employment for monks. Barbo died as a saintly bishop, and historians have never joined his name with those of Peter Damian, Stephen Harding and Bernard as a great reformer. Yet no monk since St Bernard has had a wider or more lasting influence on the forms and pursuits of the monastic life. The framework of the constitutions of Sta Giustina remained as a model for two centuries, and in ways both clear and hidden Barbo's conception of the spiritual life was a principal link in joining the spirituality of the Rhineland and Low Countries to the reviving forces of the religious orders in the Spanish counter-reformation. The reform of Sta Giustina spread gradually throughout Italy, and after it reached Monte Cassino in 1504 that mother-abbey gave its name to the whole congregation. At the end of the fifteenth century its influence spread to Spain, and guided the fervent reformed congregation of Valladolid, to which the venerable abbey of Montserrat added itself in 1497. There, early in the sixteenth century the celebrated abbot Garcia de Cisneros composed his *Exercise of the spiritual life* which was a forebear, though it did not directly inspire, the *Spiritual Exercise* of St Ignatius of Loyola. Sta Giustina had an influence also in France, where the ancient abbey of Chézal-Benoît adopted its constitutions (1488), but this and the contemporary reform of Cluny were thwarted first by the encroachments of royal power and later by the wars of religion.

A century later than the reform of Sta Giustina and the union of Bursfeld, but before the reforming decrees of the Council of Trent had been framed, a reform of another kind altogether was accomplished by Louis de Blois (1506–66), known universally by the Latin form of his name as Blosius. Louis, a native of Hainault and of distinguished ancestry, was, as a boy, page to Charles v. He entered the abbey of Liessies at fourteen, and after his studies at Ghent and

The title-page of an early French translation (1576) of the *Speculum Spiritale* (Mirror of the Soul) of Louis de Blois, abbot of Liessies (1506–66).

Louvain was chosen as coadjutor by his abbot, who died almost immediately. Left at twenty-four as abbot of a lukewarm community, his first efforts at reform proved too violent, and it was some years before a series of controversies ended with Louis in charge of a community prepared to live a regular, if not an austere, life. For them he drew up statutes and wrote a spiritual directory. The life he proposed was a monastic regime adapted to the new age of social habits. The common life was rigorously enforced for all; there was no pocket money and no private service of food; the enclosure was strictly kept and visits and journeys outside were reduced to a minimum. There was a generous allowance of recreation, when conversation, walking, music and amateur gardening were allowed. Meat was permitted, and fasting and abstinence was restricted to little more than the (then considerable) amount nominally imposed upon all Catholics by ecclesiastical law. The midnight office gave place to early morning matins. Louis de Blois thus established for his monks the framework of a regular life for all to observe, and declared his hopes that many would refrain from making use of parts, at least, of the liberty he had allowed, and his spiritual teaching, which he himself practised with a zeal that bordered upon sanctity, guided his monks towards the evengelical following of Christ. Liessies under Blosius stands with Wearmouth under Ceolfrid, Bec under Anselm and Clairvaux under Bernard as a notable instance, and an example to many, of a particular interpretation of the rule of St Benedict, and Liessies is in many ways the first abbey of the post-Renaissance cultured society of Europe, differing little from great abbeys of the modern world such as Solesmes and Maredsous. Blosius's abbey lived on, inspiring a few others but never leading a congregation, and was still fervent at its suppression in 1790.

In France, where there was something of a religious revival when the Hundred Years War finally ended, monastic life was slow to recover from destruction and dispersal. Moreover the Pragmatic Sanction of Bourges (1438) and eighty years later the Concordat of 1516, left great power to the monarchy, which could in effect control abbatial elections and use the practice of *commendam* as freely as in the fourteenth century. For this reason the attempts at reform that promised well came to nothing, and were finally extinguished by the civil war of religion.

11 The reformation: collapse and recovery

Monasticism in western Europe, spiritually weak as it was and shackled both by its roots in landed wealth and by its close dependence upon monarchs and nobles through the system of *commendam*, was in no good case to weather the unexpected storm of the Reformation. Besides the primeval charges of laxity and failure to keep the rule, the Reformers developed two new heads of attack, both of them first voiced clearly by Wyclif in England a century earlier. The one was a theological attack on the very principle of monasticism. The only Christian rule of life was the gospel; all else was merely human, and in fact evil. The monks erred in teaching that salvation lay in fasts, penances and set prayers, rather than in the simple, basic gospel virtues. Moreover, the monastic vows of chastity and obedience were contrary both to Christian liberty and to human fulfilment. Secondly, the monks were drones in society, spending money on their own comfort and doing no work of any social value. They were in possession of vast estates and other sources of wealth which would be better used if they were confiscated and distributed for schools, charities or public needs of the monarch.

We are not concerned to discuss these arguments, still less the complicated and difficult question of the extent of moral laxity among the religious of this or that region or order. The verdict of unprejudiced historians at the present day would probably be – abstracting from all ideological considerations for or against monasticism – that there were far too many religious houses in existence in view of the widespread decline of the fervent monastic vocation, and that in every country the monks possessed too much of wealth and of the sources of production both for their own well-being and for the material good of the economy. In such a state of things, existent over such wide areas, all instances in the story of the past show that rarely if ever do the goodwill and wisdom exist in all parties that might be capable of effecting a radical yet reasonable reform that would ruthlessly cut out all the dead wood without tearing the tree up by the roots. In the sixteenth century the combination of a church sick in head and members with the existence of a body of powerful and purposeful reformers, unshackled by a respect for tradition, was complicated still further by the birth-pangs of nationalism all over Europe and by a vast international dynastic conflict of which the Habsburgs were the centre.

The widespread destruction that followed showed different patterns in different regions. In Germany and Switzerland there was no systematic dissolution and little direct personal violence. Decadent monasteries, and those in or near cities that took up with Lutheran or other 'reformed' teaching, collapsed through the departure of their inmates, while others were confiscated by municipal authority. By and large monastic life adapted itself to the principle by which the ruler determined the religion (*cujus regio illius religio*) in a mosaic of petty states. Monks remained under Catholic princes or communes and disappeared elsewhere. This meant in practice that the northern half of Germany lost most of its monasteries, while the south, though devastated by the Peasants' Revolt, emerged with many of its abbeys standing. In Scandinavia the process was more gradual. In Sweden surrender to the king, Gustavus Vasa, resulted in a slow confiscation of estates over several decades, and in Norway and Denmark also there was a slow winding up. Bohemia had already lost many monasteries in the wars waged by the followers of John Hus against the Catholic crusaders; Hungary had been invaded by the Turks; in Holland and the modern Belgium the monks went from the Lutheran districts, and in the Low Countries in general many monasteries lost their wealth and independence when numerous new Catholic bishoprics were founded in abbeys. In England the monasteries went down violently between 1535 and 1540, and in Ireland a few years later.

Part of a print of 1564 showing scenes from the last days of monks of the London Charterhouse, executed in 1535 for refusing to take the oath of Royal Supremacy. The artist, apparently Italian, shows the monks tied to pillars or in stocks at Newgate, being drawn to Tyburn, and being quartered, with their entrails burning and their quarters parboiled.

In Scotland, where the scourge of *commendam* had borne most heavily, laicisation took place slowly for fifty years. Altogether, it has been estimated that in Europe as a whole something more than half the Benedictine abbeys disappeared.

France, here as in other ways, held a position apart from the Lutheran lands on the one hand, and the Italian and Iberian states on the other. The church had been saddled, on the very eve of the Lutheran explosion, with a concordat (1516) between Francis I and Leo X which gave abbatial elections almost entirely to the king, and in the event he often appointed secular prelates and lay courtiers. The situation was rendered still worse by violent governmental attempts at disciplinary reform, and many houses sought and achieved secularisation. There were very few thoroughly observant monasteries, and over all there broke the wars of religion (1562–93) in which Huguenots and others sacked and burnt many abbeys. Nevertheless, very few monks actually defected to the Reform.

The dissolution of the monasteries in England is of interest as being a topic on which, after centuries of polemic and rhetoric, there is now almost complete agreement among scholars of all allegiances. It was a large undertaking, carried through with remarkable despatch. There were in 1535 some 800 religious houses of all kinds and sizes in England and Wales. A few were enormously wealthy in both land and treasures; a few were below subsistence level; of the others, many were more than comfortably off. Altogether, their net income considerably exceeded the annual income of the Crown, that is, of the king and his government. The deviser and engineer of the exercise was Thomas Cromwell, who had recently succeeded Wolsey as the king's all-powerful minister, and who was anxious to find funds for royal expenses and for the defence of the realm. Henry VIII offered no opposition, partly because he needed money, partly because he had lately broken with Rome and had

met with opposition to his 'divorce' from some of the religious. The move was made easier by continental precedent, by sympathy for Lutheranism in London and some high clerical and government circles, and by the tepid condition of many monasteries added to a few patches of scandal. Having ascertained by enquiry the financial resources of all the houses, and having bound all abbots and monks by oath to accept the king as supreme Head of the Church, Cromwell deployed a visitation which was intended to reveal monastic weakness, foment discontent and hinder recruitment. Before the visitors had finished their task, their findings, with the good omitted and the evil inflated, were laid before Parliament, and an Act of March, 1536, suppressed houses with incomes less than £200 p.a., the sum reckoned as the minimum needed for a community of thirteen, the canonical number. In fact, no existing machinery could have absorbed all the monasteries, and universal suppression at a single blow would probably have caused widespread disturbance. As it was, the suppression helped to touch off the northern rebellion and when this was put down several abbeys, whose abbots were alleged to have abetted the rebels, went down with it. The friars were then given the illusory alternative of strict reform or surrender, and the greater abbeys were jockeyed into submission by cajolery or threats, as well as by the bribery or removal of their abbots. All was over by March 1540, and there was little resistance. The rare monastic martyrs were those who had refused to acknowledge the royal supremacy in 1535–6; the remainder, having once taken the oath, had no legal foothold against the Supreme Head.

There is general agreement today that examples of depravity were not notably more common than in the past century, that the gentry and rural population were rarely hostile and often well disposed towards the monks, and that the suppression proceeded on inequitable and often forcible lines, but examples of judicial murder and cruelty were rare, and the actual dissolution was performed as a matter of routine business. Small pensions were given to all who caused no trouble, and large allowances to the superiors who, in the eyes of the law, were the owners of the property. It is still a matter of debate whether the annuity given to the rank and file (and in particular to the nuns) was a living wage. That it rapidly decreased in real value was due to the great price rise, not to the government. In the event, most of the ordained religious picked up livings, chaplaincies and other posts in the neighbourhood of their monasteries. A proportion, but not a majority, married. Abbots and priors as a rule either became bishops or deans or retired with a manor house and a small estate. Movables, lead, etc., were sold or melted down on the spot; the estates went into the newly established Court of Augmentations (sc. of the Crown revenues); jewelry to the king's treasury. The only benefit accruing to the church or education was the establishment of five new cathedrals and two colleges; both the latter and one of the former were soon in turn suppressed.

Fifty years ago it was widely held that most of the lands were squandered as gifts and bribes on courtiers, royal agents and members of both houses of parliament. In fact, not more than three per cent went by way of gift. For the rest a market was opened at once, and though there was no lack of applicants, the flood of land did not take the bottom out of the market. Cromwell's plan was certainly to capitalise the wealth and not to sell on a vast scale, but his disgrace in 1540 led to the abandonment of his policy, and sales continued for the rest of the century. Thus the Crown whittled away its new wealth by immediate spending, and lost its unique opportunity to become independent of parliament and any popular resentment against taxation, while on the other hand the buyers, largely government men or members (often cadets) of families already owning land, rapidly added to a growing class that swayed national feeling and demanded parliamentary control of national policy.

Anglo-Saxon historians have always shown themselves insular in their treatment of the sixteenth century, and popular writers have sometimes given the impression that monasticism as an institution disappeared in Europe at the Reformation to reappear at some undefined moment of the romantic revival. Actually, the number of monks in what had been Roman Christendom was little more than halved, and there is no reason to suppose that what remained was the weaker half. It is however true that in the first half of the sixteenth century the monastic order was badly under the weather. Some of the most celebrated abbeys had ceased to be, the monastic ideal was being attacked from Christian pulpits all over northern Europe, and the forces of conservatism, slow to rally, did not put the extension of the monastic life among their priorities.

The tide of monasticism had thus reached a low ebb when the Council of Trent, in its last session, arrived at a consideration of the religious life. In earlier sessions pessimists among the fathers had even considered the complete suppression of the monastic orders. When legislation came it was, as in most other matters, conservative. The age of sixteen, preceded by a year's noviciate, was required for a valid profession; the complete common life was prescribed and the 'wages system' and private savings (*peculium*) were condemned. This and other decrees would only, in the nature of things, take effect if or when a reforming abbot and new hope had taken root within monastic circles. The same may be said of the reiteration of the Lateran legislation of 1215 and that of Benedict XII of 1336. To these the Council added a decree that the exempt monasteries of a region or province must group themselves into a congregation with chapters and regular visitations.

In the event, a reforming spirit and hopeful leaders appeared among the other signs of life in the Catholic reaction, and a gradual revival took place. Those who wished to follow the spirit of the Trent decrees had before their eyes the (Cassinese) congregation of Sta Giustina, and several bodies organised themselves upon that model and assumed the full canonical position now accorded to the congregational pattern. Others, while accepting the disciplinary regulations of Trent, were unwilling to submerge the individual house and monk in the congregation, as did the Cassinese congregation and its imitators, and looked rather to the Bursfeld model of autonomous houses held together by a general chapter with an abbot-president. As Italy and Spain were largely uninfluenced by the spirit of revival or the need for further centralisation, the new models appeared mainly in France and Germany, and broadly speaking the French revivals followed the Paduan (Cassinese) model, while those in German lands followed Bursfeld.

In the German-speaking lands that had remained Catholic there was a considerable revival of prosperity in the old congregations and a plentiful crop of new bodies, some of them confined to small areas. Though the monastic body produced few men of outstanding genius or sanctity, and therefore has made little impact on the minds of historians, German monks by their administration, learning and observance helped in the life of what were then and still remain some of the most devoutly Catholic regions of Europe. The splendour and beauty of their baroque architecture is only now winning recognition from travellers and historians of art.

In France there were several attempts, some of them successful, to establish regional congregations, but they were hindered by the prevailing system of royal *commendam*, which even Trent had failed to abolish, and also by the unwillingness of many bishops to allow abbeys to slip out of their canonical control into the exemption of an established congregation. France, however, under the rule rather than owing to the efforts of Henry IV, entered upon a golden age of religious expansion and fervour, and in the monastic sector this age dawned with the birth of the congregations of St Vanne and St Maur.

The establishment of the congregation of St Vanne of Verdun was largely due to the efforts of a saintly and eminent monk, Dom Didier de la Cour (1550–1623), who had lived for almost a quarter of a century a life of monastic perfection at St Vanne, then a house of mediocre observance. The bishop of Verdun, Prince Erric de Vaudémont, commendatory abbot of St Vanne, had endeavoured without success to reform the house until in 1598 Didier became prior. Assisted by the bishop and with papal support he began to build up a new community, and in 1604 the congregation of St Vanne was established and spread rapidly in a dozen neighbouring monasteries. Lorraine was then not part of the kingdom of France, but several French monasteries joined the reform. The constitution of the body was modelled on that of Sta Giustina. Sovereign

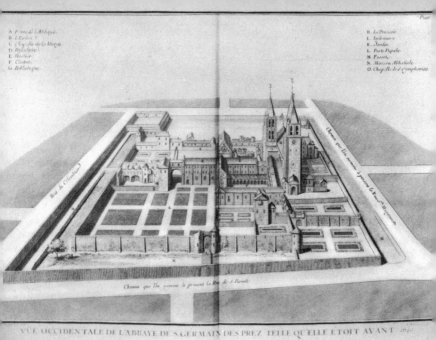

Chemin qui l'on nomme à present la Rue de S. Benoît.

VUE OCCIDENTALE DE L'ABBAYE DE S. GERMAIN DES PREZ TELLE QU'ELLE ÉTOIT AVANT

power lay with the general chapter, composed of the superior and a delegate from each house, together with the official 'visitors', under the chairmanship of the president. The last-named was elected (or re-elected) annually by chapter, which also appointed heads of houses for a quinquennium. As almost all the abbeys were held *in commendam* the superiors were usually priors. The monks took vows to the congregation and could be sent to any house. Great emphasis was laid upon the monastic training in the noviciate, and upon study and literary occupation as the normal 'work' of a monk in the modern world. Dom Didier's saying: 'An ignorant Benedictine is a nondescript (*un bénédictin ignorant est un être indéfinissable*)', was the 'power-idea' of the Vannists and Maurists, and the origin of the adjective 'learned' as the characterising adjective (*epitheton constans*) of a Benedictine monk. The congregation came ultimately to comprise some fifty houses in Lorraine, Franche-Comté (then Spanish) and Champagne (France); its offshoots in central France were separated from it, as we shall

The abbey of St Germain des Prés seen from the west as it was before 1640. The house became the centre of the Congregation of St Maur in 1651: here Dom Luc D'Achery collected a library where Mabillon, Martène, Ruinart, Montfaucon and others worked. Mabillon is buried in the church under a stone bearing no inscription beyond his name.

see. Besides personal literary work, the monks taught schools and evangelised desolate regions; they were besides in the mid seventeenth century in close touch with the currents of mystical piety described by Henri Bremond. Despite the saying of Dom Didier, the Vannists produced few scholars of the highest class, partly no doubt on account of their situation in provinces which lacked an intellectual centre and recruiting ground comparable to Paris or even Louvain. Dom Calmet, historian of Lorraine and commentator on the rule of St Benedict, is perhaps their sole representative among the immortals.

The congregation of St Maur, fairer daughter of a fair mother, came into being through an alliance of the Vannist houses that had been founded in the neighbourhood of Paris. The cause of this was largely political, and lay in the dislike of the French government and official class for any kind of dependence on a foreign authority. The new congregation came into being in 1618 and was soon joined by celebrated abbeys such as Corbie, Mont S. Michel, Bec and S. Remy at Reims. Taking the Vannist constitutions, it altered and added to them in the course of time. Its peculiar character and achievement were due largely to the vision of its first superior-general, Dom Gregory Tarrisse. Tarrisse (b. 1575) is one of the most striking examples in history of a 'late vocation'. First a soldier and then a notary, he became a priest at forty. Obtaining a benefice which was canonically monastic, he became a monk indeed and conceived the idea of a monastic reform. Professing with the Maurists in 1624 at the age of forty-nine, he soon held office and was elected superior-general in 1630, holding office till his death in 1648. Making St Germain-des-Prés the headquarters of the congregation, he provided his monks with sound constitutions which were a wisely revised version of that of the Vannists, two of the principal innovations being the re-eligibility of the triennial superior-general (as against the single year of the Vannists) and the triennial (as against annual) chapter-general, supported by an annual diet of the principal officials. He also divided the congregation into provinces. Besides this, he established study, and in particular historical study, widely understood, as the principal work of the Maurists, though he did not discontinue the Vannist legacy of teaching and preaching missions. Favoured by the establishment of headquarters, both for government and for literary work, in a capital city which was the cultural centre of Europe in an era of French history that was rich in the birth of genius and talent, the Maurists were also favoured by their excellent organisation and the recruitment of a series of men of exceptional ability, such as D'Achery, Mabillon and Montfaucon, but any similar body of its size and situation must necessarily have attracted what national talent there was for monastic studies. In the late seventeenth century there were some three thousand five hundred monks in the congregation; clearly they were not all scholars, actual or potential, but Tarrisse had laid down a programme that made full use of any material that was forthcoming. He had established for the young monks, following upon the usual courses of philosophy and theology, a study of the classics of history, and priors everywhere were ordered to propose subjects for study to their promising young monks. Besides this, he gave orders for the building up of a working library at St Germain and of lesser collections at all other houses. At Paris the monks were soon given facilities at the Royal Library and those of Colbert and others. Much of this organisation was the work of Dom Luc d'Achery (1609–55), who built up the library and initiated the Sunday afternoon reunions of scholars in his room. He was also the patron and director of the young Mabillon. Jean Mabillon (1632–1700) was not only the greatest of a great age of historical scholars, but also the embodiment of an ideal monk-scholar. Along with Bede the Venerable and Anselm of Bec he would be one of the half-dozen individuals whom all would choose

D.JOANNIS MABILLON
Presbyteri & Monachi Benedictini
CONGREGATIONIS S. MAURI
PRÆFATIONES
IN ACTA SANCTORUM ORD. S. BENEDICTI
Nunc primùm conjunctim editæ.

EJUSDEM

DISSERTATIONES V.
I. DE PANE EUCHARISTICO AZYMO ET FERMENTATO
II. DE CULTU SANCTORUM IGNOTORUM *edit. secund. cui accessit*
EPISTOLA AD STEPHANOTIUM *nunquam antea typis descripta.*
III. DE VETERIBUS RELIQUIIS DISCERNENDIS.
IV. DE VOCIBUS MISSÆ ET COMMUNIONIS IN REGULA
S. BENEDICTI ADHIBITIS.
V. DE PRIMARIO ROMARICI MONTIS INSTITUTO.

TRIDENTI MDCCXXIV.
Apud Joannem Baptistam Paronum Typogr. Episc.
PRÆSIDUM PERMISSU.

Title-page of a selection (1724) of Mabillon's writings. The prefaces to the six volumes of lives of early medieval Benedictine saints (1668–80) are brilliant historical essays. The five dissertations were originally Appendices to his *Annals*, etc. No. II is his attack on the distribution, as martyr-relics, of miscellaneous human and other remains from the Roman catacombs.

to form the composite portrait of the typical (or perhaps rather of the best type of) cloistered Benedictine. Sane, humble, devout, observant, lovable and beloved, he was also the father of scientific medieval history and palaeography, and his *Annals* and *Lives of the Benedictine Saints* laid the foundations of the critical history of the dark ages and of the religious revival of the eleventh century.

At least half-a-dozen other Maurists were in the very first rank of scholars. Martène, commentator on the rule of St Benedict, Ruinart, editor of the lives of the early martyrs, Blampin and Constant, editors of the text of Augustine's works which is still the only complete critical edition, Montfaucon, creator of Byzantine palaeography, stand near Mabillon, and innumerable others were of unusual competence. The Maurist programme which had been outlined by d'Achery as the history of monasticism and its saints – a programme excellently carried out by Mabillon – gradually extended itself to embrace all church history, local history and French history. In the eighteenth century the great plant was producing the *Gallia Christiana* – lists of all bishops, abbots and church dignitaries of France from the earliest times – the literary history of France which is still in progress, editions of the Greek fathers and a vast project of editions of medieval chronicles, together with histories of provinces and dictionaries. Besides a whole library of printed volumes, the Maurists left mountains of transcripts and notes, now in the national or departmental archives, which scholars continue to exploit.

It is natural to ask how many of the Maurist monks were scholars. A well-informed contemporary of Mabillon's lifetime put the number of whole-time publishing scholars at forty out of over three thousand religious. Even granted that the first figure is too small the opinion at least shows that academic qualifications were not thought to be an essential part of a Maurist vocation. Teaching and giving missions were always works carried on by the congregation. Nevertheless the numbers employed in the various processes of amassing material and printing the books must have been very considerable, and we may remind ourselves that there was plenty of scope for monastic vocations of other kinds among the Benedictines who were neither Vannists nor Maurists and among the numerous Cistercians. However we regard it, the Maurist congregation for some seventy years (1650–1720) is one of the 'golden epochs' of Benedictine history, though it must be remembered that some of its circumstances and characteristics – its pronouncedly congregational organisation, which left no place for the paternal abbot; its strongly academic interests; and its puritanical ascesis, which gave it a certain kinship with Port Royal, the Jansenist stronghold – set it on the margin, rather than at the centre of traditional Benedictine life.

All those familiar with church history in eighteenth-century France find themselves taken aback by the apparently sudden change from the warmth and enthusiasm and deep spirituality of the seventeenth century to the chill and aridity and bitter feuds of the epoch that followed so soon. Jansenism, the intellectual climate of the *philosophes* and Deists, the anti-clerical Voltairean hostility, the activity of European freemasonry, all combined to alter the quality of religious, and of monastic, life shortly after the death of Louis XIV. The congregations of both St Vanne and St Maur suffered from the malaise of the times. The Vannists were for some time active fellow-travellers with the Jansenists and were later deeply infected with Voltairean rationalism. The Maurists were even more sympathetic to Jansenism; they resisted the papal condemnation and came near to suppression. The congregation was divided against itself and regular observance was relaxed. It was in this climate of division and philosophic naturalism that a wholly secularist spirit came to control government circles. This led to the appointment of a hostile Commission of Regulars (1765–68), and as a result of its findings all monasteries with less than nine religious were suppressed. This move, which will remind all those familiar with English history of the Act of 1536 suppressing the lesser monasteries, resembled that Act also in covering deep hostility with a veneer of good sense. Together with another regulation raising the age of profession from sixteen to twenty-one, it had the effect of drying up recruitment and raising the average age of communities. Applied to all regulars and followed by the suppression of the Jesuits, it was a blow under which the monastic order staggered and might well have ultimately succumbed. As it was, it speedily received the *coup de grâce* of the Revolution.

Anti-clerical satire: monk before
and after the French Revolution.
A late eighteenth-century caricature
in the Bibliothèque Nationale, Paris.

Jadis je fut un bon gros Moine   Comme le Porc de St Antoine
Plein d'alimens jusques au Cou   Mais je suis aujourdhui maigre come un Coucou.

Meanwhile the German-speaking monks had been receiving doses of a similar medicine from the hands of 'enlightened despots'. While never approaching the fame of the Maurists, the German monks had remained more traditional in outlook and had escaped Jansenist influence. Germany alone had around one hundred and fifty abbeys in 1750. Thenceforward rationalism attacked them from within and governments from without. Many houses were degraded into collegiate establishments, and Maria Theresa lifted the age of profession to twenty-four and set a limit to the size of many houses. Her son Joseph II (1780–90), suppressed the contemplative orders and houses with few religious. In these ways Austria lost one-third of its monasteries and discipline and observance were ruined by regulations such as that of personal pensions and of the state education of young monks.

It was upon a Benedictine monachism thus starved of liberty and spiritual nourishment that the storm of the Revolution broke and was followed at once by the cyclone of Napoleonic domination. France, Germany and Switzerland suffered worst. It has been calculated that by 1807 all save a round dozen of abbeys in Germany had been suppressed. Those of France and the Low Countries had gone earlier. Individuals had taken refuge in other countries, and there had been wholesale defection and secularisation. Nevertheless, an historian may be allowed to regard it as dramatically fitting that the superior-general of the Maurists should be among the victims of the massacre at the Carmelite monastery in Paris, while the superior-general of the strict observance of Cluny was guillotined for saying Mass illegally.

The tide of secularisation had swept over the Alps, and in the latter half of the eighteenth century a mixture of Jansenism and rationalism had filtered into the northern half of Italy from France and Austria. Venice, Tuscany and Naples established measures limiting the freedom and recruitment of the religious orders, and the notorious synod of Pistoia (1786), while retaining the Benedictines alone of all the orders, hedged the permitted institute around with a number of regulations which in practice, had they ever been applied, would have proved intolerable. In the event, the cataclysm followed almost immediately, and between 1807 and 1811 practically all Italian monasteries ceased to exist, though a few, and among them Monte Cassino, remained as repositories of national archives, with laicised communities. The Spanish monasteries were suppressed by Joseph Bonaparte in 1809. Thus at the height of the Napoleonic domination of Europe an almost clean sweep had been made of the Benedictine abbeys, completing for the southern half of the continent the work begun by the Reformers in the north. In 1810 there were fewer monasteries in existence in western Europe than at any time since the age of St Augustine.

By a strange irony of history, among the few survivors from the general holocaust were the small groups of Englishmen who for two centuries had been outlawed, proscribed, imprisoned and in a few cases executed as criminals in their native land. Among the Catholic exiles in the reign of Elizabeth I were some who had taken monastic vows in Italian and Spanish monasteries. These had been allowed with papal approval to enter England as missionary priests. Meanwhile fresh recruits had joined the order, and in 1604 a house under the jurisdiction of the Spanish congregation of Valladolid was established at Douai, then in the Spanish dominions. It was followed by others at Dieulouard (Lorraine) and Paris, and in 1607 two novices were clothed with the monastic habit by Sigebert Buckley, the last surviving monk of the community of Westminster refounded by Queen Mary. After many negotiations the scattered groups were united (1619) in a congregation which, through the medium of Buckley, was declared by Rome to be a revival of the pre-Reformation black monk congregation. Its constitution, based on that of Valladolid, which was itself an adaptation of that of Sta Giustina, established as sovereign the quadriennial chapter, but the effective ruler of the congregation was the president, to whom all professions were made, and whose task it was to supply the mission field in England with workers. As the great majority of the chapter-members were appointed by co-option, the regime was in effect an oligarchy with a Doge at its head. The body thus formed settled down to a rhythm which it maintained for two centuries, conducting schools for the sons of Catholics in England or in exile, and supplying missionary priests (usually for life) to the chaplaincies and other stations up and down England which were allotted, by custom or authority, to Benedictines. Living thus on foreign soil with an apostolic work of great importance, the four English houses (Lamspring, in the Rhineland, the fourth, ceased to exist in the nineteenth century) lived to themselves, uninfluenced alike by the glory of the Maurists or the attacks of Jansenism and atheism. Exiles at the Revolution they were received into England in the wave of humanitarian and anti-revolutionary fervour that prevailed, and in due time were to grow into large and prosperous abbeys.

12 The Cistercians 1350–1800

We have seen the gradual decline in austerity and in some of the original characteristics of the Cistercian order that had taken place by the middle of the fourteenth century. In particular, the class of lay-brothers had all but disappeared in England and much of France before 1400, owing to the rise of the labouring class in economic prosperity and the change in agrarian policy of the monks from a regime of exploitation to one of leasing their properties. A similar rhythm was visible elsewhere, as in the Rhineland, though here it was partly due to *commendam* which took all responsibility for the land out of the hands of the monks. In central Europe, on the other hand, where the social and economic conditions of the labouring classes did not improve, there was still a modest intake of lay-brothers, though throughout Europe as a whole the striking differences of vocation between the black monks and the white tended to disappear.

Whereas the Benedictines were affected very little by the Great Schism (1378–1417), the Cistercians received great and lasting injury. Many monasteries had been pillaged by the English and *condottieri* in France; the whole machinery of the order was dislocated by war and schism; Cîteaux, the seat of general chapter, was in the Avignon allegiance, whereas Italy and England were of the Roman party. Innumerable links of filiation were broken, and the Roman allegiance held its own general chapters. Difficulties of communication, and the new national sentiment, gave rise to chapter-meetings at national or regional level, while in France and Italy the houses were afflicted with the scourge of *commendam*. Efforts at reform led to the foundation of regional or austere congregations, which threatened the essential unity of the whole body.

The Reformation eliminated the white monks and black alike from most of northern Europe. In France and Italy efforts at Cistercian reform continued. One such, taking its name from the abbey of Feuillants near Toulouse (1577), pushed austerity beyond bearable limits – the monks for some time slept on boards, fasted all Lent on bread and water, and drank from skulls – but lasted for more than a century in modified form. Germany was more fortunate in retaining something of primitive simplicity and observance, but the fragmentation of the order in Europe led to the eclipse of general chapter, the keystone of the original constitution.

Meanwhile the post-Trent spirit of reform brought a more balanced return to the past in the party of the so-called Strict Observance, which appeared in several centres in 1605 and aimed at an exact restoration of the Charter of Charity and the early decrees of chapter. Unfortunately, a series of bitter controversies in France, the seat of the reform, partly caused by the ambitions and intrigues of the political cardinals La Rochefoucauld and Richelieu, rent the Cistercian body for more than fifty years, and though the only essential difference between Strict and Common Observance lay in the matter of perpetual abstinence from meat, all attempts to establish a permanent settlement, either by restoring or by dividing the unity of the order failed, despite repeated papal intervention. At last in 1683 a compromise was agreed, and two independent Observances formed a single Order till the Revolution.

At one point in the long dispute the leader of the strict party was Armand de Rancé (1626–70). It is noteworthy that the three great reformers of French Cistercian life, at Feuillants, La Charnoye and La Trappe, were all 'convert' commendatory abbots of their houses, zealous to give to others the strong medicine they had taken themselves. Rancé, abbot of La Trappe from childhood, a converted libertine who took the habit when he was already forty years old, devoted his life to imposing upon his subjects his conception of the Cistercian life. His own past, his own character and the religious climate of the age in France which, with all its admirable

Left Portrait of the enigmatic abbot of La Trappe, Armand de Rancé (1626–70), by Hyacinthe Rigaud (1654–1743).

Right This painting by Zurbarán, said to show an episode in the relations between St Hugh of Grenoble and the monks of the Grande Chartreuse, is wholly anachronistic as an historical study, but does give an almost photographic illustration of a bishop in a Spanish Carthusian refectory of the mid-seventeenth century. Francisco de Zurbarán (1598–1664) delighted in painting Carthusians with their off-white habits.

qualities, was tinged with a strange blend of pessimism and rigorism, led him to see the monastic life as a life of penance, austerity and expiation. In consequence, he made of La Trappe a training-ground for penitential athletes, cutting away every kind of physical and spiritual satisfaction. Rancé defies appraisal. Supremely self-confident and to all appearances either strangely obtuse or capable of complete self-deception, he nevertheless died an abbot of zeal and a leader who inspired others to lives of spiritual heroism, and his work lived on to revivify the whole order. A permanent storm-centre in contemporary monastic life, *L'abbé tempête* attacked impartially Jesuits, Carthusians and Benedictines. His assault on the Maurist ideal of humanity and learning must stand beside the duel between Bernard and Peter the Venerable as one of the great monastic controversies, and he met more than his match in the slow-moving but invincible Mabillon. He remains an enigma: irrational, unchristian as we may think, but dominating the religious world of his day. La Trappe, by papal permission, stood by

itself: Rancé could contemplate and hail his abbey as the sole authentic Cistercian house. In thirty years it had grown from ten monks to three hundred, and the abbot's description of the edifying deaths of many of his sons became one of the the classics of French spirituality.

The two centuries of French preponderance in Europe had, as we have seen, periods of splendour and periods of disaster, with more than one distressing controversy. The Vannists, the Maurists and the Trappists must attract the notice of every historian. Yet we may feel that none of these are exactly central in the tradition of their order. The constitutional framework of Maurists and Vannists, and the fierce puritanism of the Trappists, admirable as they may be in the context of their times, lack both the simplicity and the spiritual breadth of a Bec or a Clairvaux. It is well to remember that alongside of these bodies there were numerous houses, both black and white, that followed, with greater or less fidelity, a more traditional path. France, indeed, in the century between 1650 and 1750, must have contained almost as many conventual houses as in the middle ages.

We may note that in these centuries the buildings were as untraditional as their inhabitants. Whether they occupied medieval sites or not, all were built or rebuilt in the style of the age, which spread gradually, with minor national differences, over the whole of Europe north of the Alps. In this style habitable buildings of every kind – house, hospital, palace, prison, barrack and monastery – were designed in a single idiom, and it is often impossible to tell from without what purpose the building serves. In this style the monastery became a building of several storeys, the monks occupied 'cells' or individual rooms, on the first, second, or third floor, while the rooms of assembly, chapter-house and refectory, were concealed architecturally on the ground floor. The cloister was often set within the range, and a large monastery was a group of quadrangles surrounded each by high buildings with numerous small windows. In these the traditional plan was often changed or overlaid, and the bird's-eye drawing, so beloved of seventeenth-century topographers, gives little information as to the use of the numerous courts of the vast new fabric of a Clairvaux or a Maurist house. So complete was the transformation that it took the antiquaries and architects of the romantic movement many decades to discover the genuine medieval layout of a great Cistercian abbey.

The development of monasticism in Russia followed a course entirely different from that taken in the west. The Mongol invasions of the thirteenth century destroyed most of the monasteries, which were for the most part in urban or suburban localities. The revival of the fourteenth century, which was an age of asceticism in Russia not altogether unlike that of the eleventh century in Italy, issued in three types of monk; the hermit, the member of a small colony (*scete*, *skit*), and the monk of the normal large monastery. Thenceforward many of the settlements were in remote sites in forests and distant parts of northern Russia. While some of the earlier houses had an idiorhythmic regime, there was a gradual move towards full community life, but the lack of a set rule, such as that of Benedict, or of firm constitutional government as among the Cistercians, gave the abbot a strong personal influence, not unlike that supposed in the Benedictine rule but in fact greater than that among monks of the west after the seventh century. The individual was formed not so much by the observance and customs of the monastery as by the founder or abbot who applied the observance, and already in the fourteenth and fifteenth centuries the abbot himself tended to be lost behind the spiritual father who filled for the individual the position of superior and director.

The name associated with the great expansion of cenobitic monasticism in the fourteenth century is that of St Sergius (1314–92), whose first monastery founded in 1344 in the country north of Moscow was idiorhythmic in character. In 1354, at the request of the patriarch of Constantinople, he founded the cenobitic house of the Holy Trinity in the imperial city. Sergius, though in character resembling Theodore the Studite, had some of the qualities of the contemporary spirituality of western Europe, with a history of visions and other experiences of the kind usually known as 'mystical'. It was an age of monastic saints, in which St Stephen founded a monastery in Perm (1396) and St Cyril (1337–1427) one in the

Left Portrait of St Sergius Radonezhki (1314–92) from an embroidered altar-cloth of the early fifteenth century.

Right The monastery of St Joseph at Volokolamsk, founded in the late fifteenth century by St Josif Volocky. It began its existence as a cenobitic monastery with strict observance, but with an interest in church life of the day, and became a nursery of bishops in the sixteenth century.

northern desert. At the same time Russian monks began, as Byzantine monks had never done, to engage in enterprises of preaching and cultivation as part of the contemporary spreading of the Christian faith. This led to a tension and ultimately to a parting of the ways which had some resemblance to the earlier Cluniac-Cistercian controversy of the west. In this the two leaders were the close contemporaries Josif Volocky (1439–1515) and Nil Sorsky (1433–1508). Josif, a monk in a monastery near Moscow, stood for a cenobitic regime, strict, regular and ascetic, and a life of activity and influence. He founded a large monastery at Volokolamsk, and his community became a nursery of bishops and a force in political life. Nil Sorsky, on the other hand, a man of noble birth, turned to a retired, contemplative life. He spent some time on Mt Athos, and then a period in a lonely monastery in Russia. Inheriting some of the spirit and teaching of the hesychasts, he was himself given to a life of penance and was an expounder of the mystical way, but he had an outgoing love for all Christians, whether monks, priests or layfolk, who were striving after perfection, and he was ready to accommodate fasting and penitential practices to individual needs and the demands of the climate. He was the great promoter of the

skit, a group of recluses, two or three in each division of a monastery, or living in a separate small house, and following the fully monastic life of prayer, work and silence.

Besides the difference in their attitudes to the purpose of the monastic life, the two leaders differed on the important point of poverty, which had so divided the west in the thirteenth and fourteenth centuries. Nil stood for poverty of life and simplicity of ornament, Josif for community possessions and the splendour of liturgical decor. The victory fell to Josif, and it marked an epoch in Russian monastic history. Monasteries became rich and worldly, with large estates and treasures.

The late sixteenth century was a period of monastic decline and economic prosperity, and was followed by the long controversy over ritual and liturgical changes in which many of the monks were conservatives. It became common for bishops to be appointed from among celibate priests and then given a purely formal monastic clothing and blessing, though there was a move towards higher education for monks which led to the promotion of 'learned monks' to the episcopate. This era was followed by the reign of Peter the Great, who was hostile to monks as he was to any independent church authority. A moderate revival of monasticism after his death was followed by the great secularisation of 1764, almost exactly contemporary with those in France and Austria. In this some six hundred monasteries, many of them very wealthy, went down and lost their lands and treasures to the state. Even so, nearly eight thousand monks remained.

A widespread revival took place earlier than the post-Napoleonic revival in the west. It derived principally from individuals of holy life and spiritual wisdom rather than from programmatic foundations of monasteries such as those of Solesmes and Beuron in the west. The leaders were spiritual patriarchs whose descendants have been traced for more than a century in 'genealogical tables' of influence. One of the first and greatest was Paisy Velichovsky, in religion Plato (1722–94), the inspirer of many masters of the monastic life; in the next generation Amvoisy Grenhov (1812–92) was a memorable figure, consulted by many including Soloviev, Dostoevsky and Tolstoy. In another stream of holiness were bishops who practised the monastic and Christian virtues in their dioceses; eminent among them were St Tikhon (1724–83; canonised 1860) and St Serafin (1759–1833; canonised 1903). During the nineteenth century the number of monasteries rose from 358 in 1810 to 550 in 1914, many being revivals of old suppressed houses. Even in modern times monasteries existed in remote northern regions, such as that on the Solovecki Islands in the White Sea near Archangel, which received some shells from British warships during the Crimean War.

The Revolution of 1917 and the changes that followed implied the end of monasticism as a spiritual force in Russia, and the number of houses dwindled by confiscation or desolation to a handful of moribund survivals.

At the end of the middle ages the promontory of Athos contained some twenty large cenobitic monasteries representing all the chief countries of the Byzantine empire; largest of all was the Russian monastery of St Pantelemon which long maintained its pre-eminence. Besides these were a dozen *skits*, two hundred cells, and more than four hundred hermitages. Among the large houses were several idiorhythmic ones, governed by a council of all the presidents of the small groups. All lived a life in which the Office and manual work, largely gardening, occupied most of the day; the heavier work was done by brothers. The regime was austere, and many lived lives of devoted piety. After the fall of Constantinople Athos was more than ever the refuge, the reservoir and the jewel of monastic observance for the whole orthodox church, a kind of monastic republic.

This it continued to be, perhaps with a certain fall of spiritual temperature, until very recently, and even the swelling tide of savants, biblical scholars, artists, collectors, art dealers and mere tourists did not essentially change life on the Mount, which besides being the largest monastic enclosure in the world was also probably the richest in manuscripts and treasures of art to survive into the twentieth century. Here as elsewhere 1914 was a beginning of sorrows. The Russian revolution deprived its largest monastery and many cells of their sources of recruitment and income in the homeland, and other national monasteries suffered in some measure. By the treaty of Lausanne (1926), ratified by church and state in Greece, its continuance as a monastic republic was ensured, but economic deterioration and a lack of recruits persisted, and at present the population is very small. Every effort has been made by the patriarchate of Constantinople and impoverished Greek governments, but it is hard to see how the holy mountain can ever, in the modern climate, recover to be a home and agency of monastic fervour. Elsewhere in Greece the decadence of celebrated ancient monasteries has been even more marked.

14 The revival of the nineteenth century

At the end of the domination of Napoleon I the monastic order, and in particular the traditional Benedictine family, was in worse case than at any time since the days of Benedict himself. Speaking loosely, it may be said that the Reformation had cut off all abbeys in the northern countries, and that the French Revolution and Napoleon had accounted for the rest. In some cases, indeed, the work of destruction went on, when liberal governments in Switzerland and Spain renewed the work of secularisation. It has been computed that of the thousand-odd monasteries of Benedictines and Cistercians extant in 1750 less than a dozen of the white monks and only thirty of the black monks survived. Apart from the four English houses, the rest were scattered over Bavaria, Austria and Sicily. Those hostile to the monastic way of life, and indifferent contemporaries in England or America, seemed to be justified in their opinion that monasticism, a medieval survival, had vanished forever along with the other institutions of the *ancien régime*.

The revival was not long in coming, and though it owed its origin to deeper causes, it was assisted in France and other countries by the wave of romantic interest in the middle ages, and by the sense that an imitation of medieval achievements and institutions was the best way of combating the ills of the past century. The new life sprang mainly from three sources, in France, in Italy, and in Germany. That in France was the work of Prosper Guéranger (1805–75), a secular priest who conceived of his foundation of Solesmes (Sablé par Sarthe, 1833) as a revival and a model of the age-old liturgical spirituality of the church. Solesmes became the mother-abbey of the congregation of France, which has come to include also abbeys in England, Spain, Belgium, Luxembourg, Italy, Canada, Mexico, Argentine and Martinique. Excluding all external activities, such as parochial, educational and agricultural undertakings, Solesmes has displayed a rich liturgical life and a considerable output of scholarship. The founder intended to revive the spirit of the Maurists, but in the event Solesmes and its off-spring are rather in the tradition of Bec and other great abbeys of the eleventh and twelfth centuries. Guéranger himself took an active part in the controversies that divided French Catholics in the matter of papal temporal power and papal infallibility, and aroused criticism in some quarters, but his works on the liturgy, in particular *The Liturgical Year*, were extraordinarily popular and influential in bringing his contemporaries to an appreciation of the riches of the missal and breviary. He was followed at Solesmes by musicologists and executants of genius, such as Doms Pothier and Mocquereau, who presented from the manuscripts the plain chant of the golden age (AD 600–1100) and a choral performance that was for long superior to any other and which made of Solesmes the Mecca of 'plain-chantists'. These scholars effectively rescued from oblivion the chant which had been debased and rejected for many centuries, and if some of the theory and execution that seemed unassailable has since been questioned, it is Mocquereau and Pothier who have provided material for a revision, should this prove needful. The collection and photographing of the innumerable manuscripts, the collation and assessment of the various traditions, and the constitution of a final text and its production in the form of gradual and antiphoner gave excellent and useful work for all types of talent, and when the fame of Solesmes grew there were courses of lectures and summer schools on the chant, to say nothing of the elaborate choral execution and performance for gramophone and wireless recording, when that became a possibility. Solesmes also had in Dom Pitra (1812–89), later cardinal and librarian of the Vatican, a liturgical scholar and orientalist of note, but the mother-abbey was surpassed in this field by the English house of Farnborough, founded in 1895 by the ex-empress Eugénie at the mausoleum of the ill-fated imperial dynasty. Here Abbot Cabrol, Dom Louis Gougaud and the legendary Dom Henri Leclercq, who with his own pen wrote the greater part, including every word in the later volumes, of the great *Dictionnaire d'archéologie et de liturgie chrétienne*. We may perhaps note that, whether by design or necessity, the abbey of Solesmes is architecturally wholly without the plan and appearance of a medieval abbey.

A second beginning was made in Italy, where a few monasteries of the Cassinese congregation had survived in a moribund condition. Houses were founded or refounded at Subiaco, Finalpia and elsewhere, and grouped by Pius IX into an autonomous province of the Cassinese congregation. Calling themselves 'of the primitive observance', they revived the strictly common life with the midnight office and the traditional fasts. After an attempt to carry the Cassinese houses into the reform, the new group hived off to form an independent congregation with several provinces. They were strengthened by the adherence of several notable abbeys outside Italy, including the Spanish Montserrat and the French Pierre-qui-vire. The last-named had an interesting history. Founded in 1850 by a secular priest, the Abbé Muard (1809–54), with the aim of evangelising districts lost to the faith, Pierre-qui-vire combined an austere regime (originally that of the Trappists) with an apostolic zeal. It ran into difficulties on account of its physically severe demands and finally joined the Subiaco body, in which it formed the nucleus of a French province, distinguished still by its austerity. In spite of this, indeed perhaps precisely because of its appeal to two ideals of the nineteenth century, the penitential and the missionary, the house flourished and continued to do so in the twentieth century, founding several houses with the same characteristics. The constitutions of the Subiaco congregation, which in their original form followed the pattern of Sta Giustina, with temporary abbots appointed by general chapter, and professions made to the congregation, not to the house, came under attack from the traditionalists who desired autonomy and the right of

electing an abbot for each house, and from others who saw in an international, provincialised and centralised order a kind of hybrid of Benedictine and Jesuit. Modifications were therefore made in the direction of autonomy, but the congregation remained international, with an abbot-general with universal jurisdiction.

In Germany the ancient Bavarian congregation was gradually revived by King Ludwig I and canonically restored in 1858, but the dynamic influence for Germany came from a secular priest of the Rhineland, later Dom Maurus Wolter (1825–90), who with his brother Placid took the habit at St Paul's in Rome and at the instigation of Princess Catherine of Hohenzollern refounded the abbey of Beuron, after consultation with Abbot Guéranger at

Solesmes. Beuron with its strict discipline and its accent on liturgical devotion translated Solesmes, so to say, into the German
mode. It became an archabbey on the model of Bursfeld, and its
exile under the Kulturkampf (1876–87) resulted in the foundation
of Erdington (England), Emmaus (Bohemia), Seckau (Styria) and,
on the return to Germany, Maria Laach in the Rhineland. Previously, a Belgian monk of Beuron, Dom Hildebrand de Hemptinne,
had established a house at Maredsous in Belgium, which in turn
gave birth to several daughters. During the period between 1887
and 1914, the age of Germany's expansion in so many directions,

Archabbey and College of Vincent, Pennsylvania, the first
Benedictine abbey to be founded in America (1846). The abbey
church, with basilical rank, is seen to left, with the new
monastery building at the right. The present Abbot Primate of the
Benedictine Federation is a monk of this house.

the Beuronese congregation became at once the cynosure and the
bogy of the Benedictine world. Its self-confidence and 'effortless
superiority', its expansionist outlook, and its *cachet* of discipline
and efficiency, made it the crack regiment of the Benedictine corps,
the object at once of emulation and apprehension. With Beuron,
Maria Laach and Maredsous among its houses, with its resources
of saintliness, scholarship and administrative ability, and with a
foothold in Rome, in England, and in Brazil, it seemed destined to
take in the modern world something of the place that Cluny had
taken in an earlier age. In the event, any dream there may have been
of a monastic empire vanished in the disasters of the two great wars
and the Hitler regime, leaving Beuron numerically and spiritually
healthy, but shorn of her 'colonial' foundations.

Subiaco, Solesmes and Beuron were not the only centres of
revival. In Austria a few abbeys had never ceased to function, but
it was not till 1889 that seventeen abbeys were parcelled into two
congregations. In Hungary a small congregation of five was established. In Switzerland the ancient monastery of Einsiedeln revived,
together with Engelberg, Disentis and other houses exiled in
sites in the Tyrol forming the Swiss congregation. Switzerland
during the nineteenth century was (as it still remains) the only
country of western Europe where new monastic foundations are
forbidden by law. Those that exist are therefore large communities,
and an early overflow took Swiss monks to America.

In England the communities of St Gregory at Douai and St
Laurence at Dieulouard, driven out at the Revolution, settled finally
at Downside (Somerset) and Ampleforth (Yorks) respectively.
That of St Edmund at Paris returned after Napoleon's fall to
the house of its confrères at Douai, only to be evicted once again by
the Combes law of associations in 1903, to settle at Woolhampton
(Berks). They grew slowly but steadily after Catholic Emancipation,
and during the last twenty years of the nineteenth century fought a

successful battle, largely under Downside initiative, for the restoration of autonomy and abbatial status for the individual houses.

In Spain and Portugal the monks, sorely tried and dispersed under Joseph Bonaparte, were more unfortunate than their brethren elsewhere in catching the backlash of the 'liberalism' that other countries had encountered earlier. All the monasteries of Spain, fifty-six in number, were suppressed in 1835. Montserrat, a national shrine, was soon restored, but a congregation did not come into being for fifty years.

Finally, in any survey of Europe mention should be made of the Congregation of St Ottilien, founded (1884) with the direct purpose of overseas missionary activity. It came to have two sister houses in Germany, and missionary foundations in Africa, South America and elsewhere.

Canada and the United States had no monks before the mid-nineteenth century. Then (1846) a small colony went out from the Bavarian congregation to St Vincent, (Pa), where there were thick settlements of German immigrants. St Vincent became arch-abbey of a flourishing congregation. Nine years later, when the Swiss abbeys were having trouble with cantonal governments, Einsiedeln founded St Meinrad (Ind) with the aim of evangelising the Indians. We shall return later to the two American congregations.

15 From isolation to union

Hitherto the aim of this book has been to trace in outline the history of the monastic way of life. Readers will probably have become aware that, while in the eastern church the character of monasticism has changed little, in the west there has been a steady, though by no means unbroken, development in three directions. First, the traditional, central stream in monasticism, which has come to be called Benedictine, has gradually approached, without ever attaining, the organisation of a single body or 'order'. Secondly, that this traditional monachism has widened within its bounds like a fan or the colours of the spectrum, far outside the limits of anything specified in the rule of St Benedict, so as to embrace every kind of life from the austere, fully contemplative life of the Trappist to the life of a dedicated parish priest or schoolmaster. Thirdly, that from the eleventh century onwards the monastic order, which till that time was the only form of vowed regular life for men, lost its monopoly and saw many of its 'occasional' employments and activities accepted as a principal employment or *raison d'être* by religious orders of other kinds, whether of canons or of friars. It may however be noted also that there has been a 'two-way traffic' in this matter, and that since the Reformation Benedictines have in many ways taken up into their own life what had hitherto been regarded as the characteristic work of other institutes. These three considerations may be examined a little more closely.

The constitutional history of traditional monasticism following the rule of St Benedict has developed very slowly. The rule, though certainly making allowance in more than one place for modifications in different climatic conditions, was written, so far as we know, for a single abbey (that of Monte Cassino) and applied at only one other (Terracina) by its author. Thenceforward, from 550 to 814, it spread here and there by the action of individuals, but it nowhere formed a bond of legal union. Charlemagne conceived the project of uniting all the monasteries of his empire (the modern

France, north Italy, the Low Countries, Switzerland and western and southern Germany) in an observance governed by the rule and agreed constitutions, with a central supervision directly answerable to the emperor, but the scheme was never fully applied and soon forgotten. All that survived was a sentiment of family unity. The Cluniac association, and others such as the unions of Gorze, Hirsau, Bec and Bursfeld were indeed embryo 'orders', as being groups united in a particular observance under some sort of central control, but none of these bodies, not even the vast network of Cluny, made any claim to be or wish to become a union of the whole existing body of monks.

Indeed, when the Cistercians from *c.* 1115 came to form in the Charter of Charity what was the first fully organised monastic grouping, with disciplinary interconnection and a judicial and legislative body in their general chapter, they became by this very process separated from the black monks, and despite their battle-cry of 'the rule to the last dot', by so doing they lost for ever the name 'Benedictine'. The traditional monks were bidden by Innocent III and the IV Lateran Council to unite in annual provincial chapters for disciplinary purposes, but this was largely ignored in continental Europe, and even in England there was little organisation of the modern kind; by 1400, indeed, there was in Europe as a whole far less congregational activity than the Lateran Council had decreed. Yet a few decades later, as we have seen, came the epoch-making creation of Sta Giustina of Padua, by which a fully articulated congregation was established in which supreme and overall authority lay, not with the individual abbots or an abbot-president, but the chapter, and with a committee acting for the chapter. This innovation, which removed the linch-pin of the Benedictine rule, the independent abbot, was only possible because he had been removed already by the evils of secular control and commendatory abbots, and as these abuses persisted for more than three centuries, despite the reforming activities of Trent, the congregational system remained in several countries, and in France in particular was the only means of securing domestic independence. It was not, however, universal, and in German-speaking countries the new and revived unions were on the model of IV Lateran, though somewhat more articulated and effective. All schemes of wider fusion were blocked by the nationalist policies of monarchs, the great variety of organisation among the various congregations, and the very excellence of that organisation in the case of the Maurists and others.

The French Revolution and the Napoleonic conquests, with the concomitant secularisation and suppression, left a blank sheet for the leaders of the revival to fill, but neither the fortunes of the papacy nor the politics of Europe in the first half of the nineteenth century nor the ideals of the new founders favoured an overall organisation, and in fact the new constitutional arrangements showed an even greater variety than before. There were the old regional and provincial congregations, loosely organised, as in Germany; the tightly bound but largely traditional congregations of France and Beuron, where the abbeys were domestically independent under the remote control of an abbot president; there was also the frankly international congregation of Subiaco, with semi-autonomous regional provinces which made it almost an order within an order; and finally there was a truly miniature 'order', such as that of St Ottilien, devoted to a particular external work and without local or regional associations.

As the nineteenth century wore on, two tendencies or tensions developed. On the one hand the great strengthening of central authority in the church after 1870 led to a bureaucratic desire in the Roman curia for uniformity of practice and unity of control, and under pope Leo XIII this was partially attained in the Cistercian and other orders. On the other hand the rapid development of historical studies, especially in Germany, France and England, led to a new veneration for the traditional practice and in particular for the autonomous abbey. Thus the English congregation, hitherto based on the model of Sta Giustina, secured a change to the older style of things, and within the Benedictine body several individual houses transferred themselves from a congregational to an autonomous status.

Leo XIII, who desired to bring the whole body of Benedictine monks into some sort of union, founded the great international college of Sant'Anselmo, and placed at its head an 'abbot primate' without ordinary jurisdiction over any congregation and its members, but with some powers of supervision, and the prestige of a prelate able to inform and advise the Holy See. From time to time efforts were made by Rome to increase the central powers, but they were met with the resistance of the assembled abbots, rightly jealous of traditional Benedictine autonomy, and the Code of Canon Law published in 1918, of which one of the principal editors was the Benedictine Justinian Ceredi, later primate of Hungary and cardinal, placed the individual abbot among the major superiors, equal in status to the heads of other religious orders. At last in 1964 Pope Paul VI established an international confederation of Benedictine monks which embraced also the Silvestrines and Olivetans, but which left intact the existing status and constitutions of abbots and congregations. The Benedictines, therefore, though they are of the Order (= regulated way of life) of St Benedict, are not, strictly speaking, a 'religious order' such as the Dominicans and Jesuits.

Though the normal concept and definition of a monk is of one who is living in retirement from the world, whether as a solitary or in community, and although in the first beginnings of monastic history this was borne out in fact, yet the term and the way of life were, almost from the beginning, elastic. The monks of Pachomius, though strict and quasi-enclosed, plied numerous trades, crafts and toils, and the monks of St Basil administered charitable works. In the west, the monastery was for long a family apart from the world, and neither the rule of the Master nor that of St Benedict allows for any employment that has an end or purpose outside the monastic precinct, though St Gregory in his *Dialogues* shows us St Benedict preaching to the pagans of his neighbourhood. In the centuries that followed, the typical monastery was large and complex, with numerous dependents of one kind or another – servants, officials, serfs, hired labourers – but it was still self-contained and its inmates, by and large, lived apart from the world. Their work of copying and adorning manuscripts, and of themselves composing historical or theological works, was to prove of supreme value to future generations, but of this those occupied in these pursuits saw and intended nothing.

Nevertheless, monks gradually came to take part in external activities. In the missionary work in which they achieved so much, as also in the pastoral work of individual monks who became bishops, they accomplished tasks which were not in themselves monastic, but which were Christian duties which, in the conditions of the times, could not and would not have been fulfilled by others. Considered with the hindsight of history, Augustine of Canterbury, Boniface, Ansgar, Cyril, Methodius and their companions were harbingers of the Dominicans and Jesuits, the beginning of a break-down of the then omnicompetent monastic order. There was no way of becoming a missionary without first being a monk, while on the other hand a true and tried monk could be a missionary without losing his essential monkhood. Moreover, the great missionaries took with them the monastic life to the mission-field and planted the abbeys that were to be centres of the fully monastic life for all the medieval centuries.

In other occupations, such as the promiscuous engagement in

what would now be called parochial work, or the mingling with secular life that entailed a gradual declension to the status of secular canons, the monastic life suffered. Throughout the middle ages, quite apart from the aberrations of individuals and the collapses of decadence, there were in every age, and widely in some ages, lapses of the monastic life down the scale to canonical or even to merely clerical life, and instances of the dispersal of houses into what would now be called pastoral work. These involvements and lapses have taken place in every age, not excepting our own. In part, at least, they occur because the monks of the west have from early times commonly proceeded to holy orders, and in part because the monastic life is not something different from a fervent Christian life, but a species of it.

Yet though monks at one time or another have worked for the church outside their monastery or, if remaining inside, have accomplished work, such as education, which had its end outside, there has been since the twelfth and thirteenth centuries a steady growth of religious institutes outside the cloister engaged on Christian works of preaching, evangelising, teaching, healing and the rest. These, the religious orders of canons, friars and clerks, are in a way comparable to the specialisation and proliferation of skills and occupations that occur in every complex and civilised society. The religious orders resemble the monks in their spiritual goal – the dedication to the service of God – and in some of the means of attaining it, but they differ (or should differ) by reason of their closer intercourse with the life of Christians and others who are bound by no particular engagement.

What may be called the contemporary history of the monastic orders begins in the 1890s with the mergers and other actions of Leo XIII. In the seventy years between 1890 and 1960 almost all the monastic bodies, save for a few which for centuries have lingered solely as local species, increased more swiftly than at any time since the early seventeenth century. In that space, the numbers of Benedictine and Cistercian monks and of their houses doubled, with a corresponding increase in the regions to which they had penetrated. This increase appears even more remarkable when it is remembered that during the decades of that period recruitment was at a standstill in many countries for at least ten years (during the two great wars), that in both world wars individual houses were destroyed, dispersed or displaced, and that after the second war monastic life was gradually brought to a state of near extinction in European countries under communist control. While there can be no doubt that some of the numerous recruits immediately after both wars were evidence of a reaction from the hazards and horrors of modern warfare, hot and cold, this does not explain the universal and constant increase nor the general spiritual and material well-being of almost all the bodies concerned. Moreover, the increase was ubiquitous, and was seen in the more austere and cloistered institutes, such as the Reformed Cistercians and the congregation of France, as well as in the active and missionary congregations, such as those of St Ottilien and of America. A survey of the monastic world during the first half of the present century will help us to follow this progress.

In Italy the increase has not been spectacular in the ancient Cassinese congregation, the modern descendant of Sta Giustina. The two largest houses are Monte Cassino itself and St Paul without the walls at Rome, each with a relatively small community of forty-odd, but it has continued to produce sons of distinction, among whom in recent times was Ildephonsus Schuster, abbot of

The 'upper' monastery of Subiaco, east of Rome, incorporating the cave and small monastery where Benedict lived as a hermit and later as abbot *circa* 500–25. In his day the valley was filled by an artificial lake immediately below the monastery; it was constructed by Nero whose villa (Subiaco = sub lacu = below the lake) lay further down the valley.

St Paul's and later cardinal archbishop of Milan (d. 1954). The Italian province of the Subiaco congregation is more numerous with several large houses among which are Praglia, near Venice (the largest), Monte Vergine (extra-provincial) and, somewhat paradoxically, Sta Giustina at Padua.

Of the fifteen black Benedictine congregations three stand out as representatives in different ways of traditional monastic life expressed in modern idiom: the congregations of France, Subiaco and Beuron, whose origins we have already noted. That of France, with its mother-house of Solesmes is, as might be expected, the most akin to the great medieval houses of the French and Anglo-Norman kingdoms. With a large community, all living within the orbit of the monastic life, and occupied with a number of practical and intellectual pursuits, many of them directly connected with the presentation of the liturgy, they are perhaps the central ray in the modern Benedictine spectrum – observant, regular and yet moderate, in a regime of no extreme severity, with a devotional life centred upon the choral liturgy. Solesmes, in common with other French monasteries, was hit by the Combes legislation of 1903 and went into exile, first at Appuldurcombe and later at Quarr, both in the Isle of Wight. A community, left at Quarr when the main body returned to France after the First World War, has become independent and has now an English abbot, and a largely English community. Another English foundation already mentioned, that of Farnborough, was the home of several distinguished scholars, but its particular *raison d'être* disappeared with the death of the ex-empress Eugénie, and the French monks transferred the property to Prinknash abbey. The principal continental houses of the French congregation, such as Ligugé, Ousterhout and Clervaux the monastic home of Dom Jean Leclercq, have a similar life of liturgy and study.

The Subiaco congregation, which contains more houses than any

other, and perhaps also, by a narrow margin, more religious, is in truth an order in itself. Not only is it international, with houses in every continent save north America, and provinces in almost all the countries of western Europe, but the greatest difference of observance exists between houses of different provinces and even of the same province. Thus the French province, with its chief house at Pierre-qui-vire, practises a near-Trappist regime, combined with missionary zeal, whereas the Italian province resembles several other congregations in its observance. As for the English province, it contained within living memory houses of markedly distinct nuances of spirit. Ramsgate, with a school and parishes, was externally similar to the way of life of the English congregation, while Buckfast began life as a foundation from, and temporary refuge for, the mother-house of Pierre-qui-vire, and Prinknash, originally the convert community of Caldey, with a white habit and a Cistercian simplicity of life was for many years *sui generis* in spirit. Seen as a whole, however, the congregation of Subiaco is an impressive body in the extent of its enterprises and its observance.

The congregation of Beuron, in contrast to that of Subiaco but in harmony with the national characteristics of its homeland, was for long, and still is in part, uniform in observance and, at least until the advent of national socialism, with a sense, or at least a savour, of imperialism. With several of its houses in the predominantly Catholic regions of Bavaria and the Rhineland, its estates were worked by large companies of bearded lay-brothers, simple, devout and devoted, and the monks, shaven and habited with the uniformity and spotless care of a company on parade, moved with precision through a carefully planned horarium. The almost feudal relationship of monks to brothers, and the reverence paid to an abbot (all the more fitting, it seemed, if he were also an aristocrat by birth), seemed, thirty or forty years ago, at once impressive and, in practice, oppressive. In the years before 1914 they founded houses in Belgium, England, Bohemia and elsewhere, sent a reforming colony to Brazil and established a house in Jerusalem. From 1893 to 1943 two Beuronese abbots functioned as abbots-primate at Sant'Anselmo in Rome, and gave to the college, and through the college to the Benedictine world, a character which some accepted and others withstood. In other ways also, in the loan of monks to stiffen decaying houses, and by a school of art which embellished the very heart of Benedictine tradition in the crypt of Monte Cassino, Beuronese ideals had a considerable vogue. This was inevitably reduced by the First World War. The English house of Erdington ceased to exist and several of its members joined the English congregation. More significantly, the Belgian houses petitioned Rome for separation, and became a national congregation in 1920. Reduced thus almost exclusively to metropolitan Germany, the congregation continued to flourish, but received rough treatment under the Nazi regime and during the subsequent war. It remains fervent, but has not greatly expanded, and from 1947 to 1967 Sant'Anselmo was under the rule of abbots from the Swiss congregation. Besides its exemplary observance, Beuron was in the van of the liturgical movement in what may be called its conservative and pre-vernacular phase before Vatican II, and Maria Laach, a house favoured at one time by Kaiser Wilhelm II, has during the present century stood out as a focus of liturgiology and historical research under Abbot Herwegen and Dom Odo Casel. Both these abbeys publish a series of critical and historical studies.

The most distinguished community of the Beuronese congregation after the mother-abbey before the First World War was undoubtedly the Belgian abbey of Maredsous, which rivalled Solesmes in fame and surpassed it in scholarship. Dom Hildebrand de Hemptinne its founder and first abbot (later first abbot-primate) and his successor, the Irish Dom Colomba Marmion (1858–1923), had in their community a galaxy of talent, including the English patristic and scriptural scholar Dom John Chapman, the theologian Dom Jansens, later rector of Sant'Anselmo, and the historians, Dom Ursmer Berlière, Dom Germain Morin and Dom Philibert Schmitz. Abbot Marmion himself was and is one of the most widely read spiritual writers of the present century, and his cause for beatification has been introduced at Rome. Maredsous also had an example of another kind of holiness of life in the young relative of the first abbot, Dom Pie de Hemptinne (1880–1907). Besides a school and the popularisation of liturgy, the monks of Maredsous edit and produce the learned *Revue Bénédictine*, the leading periodical on patristic literature and monastic history.

When the Belgian congregation was created Maredsous had

already founded the houses of Mont-César at Louvain and Saint-André at Bruges, worthy daughters of their mother. The former distinguished itself by a liturgical apostolate among the clergy and the historical and patristic studies of Dom Capelle, Dom Cappuyns and others, the latter by the more popular liturgical work of Dom Gaspard Lefèbvre (d. 1967) and its scriptural scholarship. In less conventional fashion Dom Lambert Beaudoin, as a crown to a career of varied and daring activities, founded at Amay what is now the abbey of Chevetogne to pave the way to reunion of the western and eastern churches. The periodical *Irenikon* is published in the abbey.

A fourth congregation on the continent of Europe was a late (1884) and untraditional newcomer to the revival of the nineteenth century. This was the congregation of St Odilia (German Sankt Ottilien) based on the abbey of that name near Augsburg. This institute, founded primarily as a training house for missionaries, adopted the Benedictine rule with its liturgical tradition as an effective and (at least to the Germany converted by St Boniface) a traditional means of spreading the message of the gospel. Between its origin and the colonial turmoil of the 1950s it had established, in addition to two more reservoir and recruiting abbeys in south Germany and Switzerland, numerous abbeys or priories in Korea, Manchuria, east Africa, Zululand and Venezuela. The two abbeys in east Africa, both abbeys *nullius* (i.e., where the abbot has full jurisdiction over a territory which is outside all diocesan control) recently contained more than two hundred monks, and before the Korean war the monks had charge of two 'apostolic vicariates' (missionary administrative districts) in Korea and Manchuria.

The English congregation from its beginning had the twofold occupation of education and missionary activity. We have seen how they returned to England as exiles during the French Revolution. In the nineteenth century they provided, besides missionary priests, a number of bishops both for the restored hierarchy of England, in which one see, that of Newport, was reserved for them, and for the British colonies (the Mauritius and Australia), but the Oxford movement and the enthusiasms of the early converts passed them by, and with their small priories, their parochial commitments and their congregational form of government they had no romantic or vocational attraction for the new generation. It was only towards the end of the century that a movement of reform, more constitutional than disciplinary, achieved a phased change-over to the traditional group of autonomous abbeys (1900). The architects of this development desired a full liturgical and monastic life, together with scope for literary and learned work such as was being achieved in the Beuron and Solesmes congregations, but Downside was in fact the only house which showed results of this kind, and the others continued to maintain and develop their parochial commitments. Concurrently, the need felt by the growing Catholic body for education of the type provided by the ever-growing class of public schools led to the rapid growth at these three houses of large schools between 1900 and 1930, thus creating a new absorbing work for the growing communities. In 1850 a monastery had been founded at Belmont (Herefordshire) to serve as a common noviciate and to provide the chapter of the pro-cathedral of the Newport diocese, with its Benedictine bishop. This became autonomous in 1915 and in turn opened a boarding school. Finally, at the beginning of the present century a monastery, founded at Fort Augustus in Scotland as an independent venture, joined the English congregation after a series of experiments and misfortunes. Like its sister houses, it had a school and parish work.

Outside Europe, the United States, and on a smaller scale Canada also, opened a new chapter in monastic history about the turn of the century. Though from the beginning of American independence complete religious freedom had been constitutionally safeguarded, the small Catholic population of the original Anglo-Saxon colonies was at first restricted to Maryland and a few of the eastern cities. In the nineteenth century, however, the first wave of immigration began, chiefly from the German-speaking lands. It was with the primary purpose of preserving the faith of these immigrants that Ludwig I of Bavaria assisted Dom Boniface Wimmer of Metten abbey to establish himself with postulants at Beatty, Pennsylvania, where the abbey of St Vincent, as we have seen, became arch-abbey of a congregation modelled originally on that of Sta Giustina-Cassino, and hence called the American Cassinese congregation. As they developed, they also took secondary and higher education as their principal work, with consider-able pastoral activity, and a particular interest at first in the negro population of Maryland. St Vincent was followed within ten years by a group of monks from Einsiedeln, who founded St Meinrad's abbey in Indiana and were later joined by a colony from Engelberg, to found a congregation on the traditional model. Their primary work was the evangelisation of the north American Indians and the staffing of episcopal seminaries. Each congregation made a foundation in Canada in the early years of the present century.

At first, and for many decades, these two American congregations bore a strong imprint from their origins, and drew their recruits either from Europe, or from the German immigrants in the USA, or from children of their own parishes. Engaged as they were in active works they remained until the First World War largely unaffected by contemporary Benedictine liturgical and scholarly interests, and with little impact on the educated classes of New England or the south. This lack of contact with Benedictine life led a convert Episcopalian and Bostonian clergyman, later Dom Leonard Sargent, to organise a foundation from the English congregation. Father Sargent professed at Downside in 1916, but when, after delays caused by the war, a start was made at Portsmouth, Rhode Island, Fort Augustus was the sponsor-abbey. A second foundation was soon made at Washington, DC, with academic and pastoral connections with the Catholic University of America. Later still, another foundation was made from England by Ampleforth at St Louis. Finally, an abbey was founded by the congregation of France in the French-speaking province of Quebec. Thus in north America the European pattern, which must seem an untidy one to ecclesiastical bureaucrats, has repeated itself. Each of the two great countries has houses of three different congregations, and each has one or more houses of European filiation.

If central and south America, though Catholic in name at least for more than four centuries, has occupied an insignificant place in Benedictine history, a principal cause may be found in the comparatively slight Benedictine influence and initiative in the first century of Spanish colonial enterprise. Only in Brazil, Mexico and Peru had any foundations been madè, and in the two latter countries they became extinct. In Brazil a Portuguese group became an independent congregation in 1827, but all recruitment was banned by an anticlerical government in 1855. In 1895 at the request of the survivors a colony of Beuronese monks was sent out from Maredsous, and a steady revival has taken place. In all the other Latin American countries the existing monasteries are dependencies or at least within the congregational control of Europe. Thus Mexico has two foundations from the Spanish house of Silos in the congregation of France; Martinique and Trinidad have houses of the French and Belgian congregations respectively, and in the latter island there is also a house of the St Ottilien monks. Venezuela has three small groups from St Ottilien; Chile has two foundations from the Spanish Subiaco house of Samos and one from Beuron; Colombia has also one from Samos. The Argentine has a large house under the Subiaco regime, a daughter house of Silos at Buenos Aires, and a small colony from Einsiedeln in the pampas. At the moment of writing (1967) a pilot group from Worth (English congregation) has gone out to Paraguay.

A distinctive and novel feature of the period 1870–1940 was the dedication of some congregations or houses to missionary work among non-European and non-Christian peoples. The activities of the professedly missionary congregation of St Ottilien have already been mentioned, as have also some isolated foundations of other houses, in particular those of Silos and other abbeys of the congregation of France. The French Subiaco house of Pierre-qui-vire had proposed missionary activities as a reason for its foundation, and had (or still has) missionary posts in Vietnam, Cambodia, Madagascar and Morocco. St André at Bruges developed a strong missionary interest, and before the recent upheavals in Africa had charge of the vicariate apostolic of Katanga (Elizabethville) in the Congo, with a second large house in the colony. Other foundations were in China, India and Angola, the last from a Portuguese abbey of the Belgian congregation. Finally, two Spanish monks, exiled in 1835, founded a monastery, Nova Nursia, in what was then the *terra incognita* of northern Australia to care for the natives. The house later joined the Swiss Subiaco congregation with the status of a missionary abbey with jurisdiction over the neighbouring district.

Thus between the mid nineteenth and the mid twentieth centuries Benedictine monachism had once more spread a network over much of Europe and had also begun to emulate the evangelising activities of the age of Boniface and Anskar. There was, however, a great difference between the earlier and the later missionary work, which recent years have continued to underline. In the conversion of Europe, Christian missionaries were preaching to those who had racial affinity and environmental similarity. Once converted to the new religion, they were able to accept easily and permanently all its institutions. In the modern world missionaries were divided from their converts by race, by background, by deep psychological and atavistic chasms, and even granted that the withdrawal and dedication of monasticism has its roots deep in the human response to an acknowledged creator and redeemer, the trappings in which this life was brought to Asian and African converts were wholly unfamiliar and, in some cases, seemingly repulsive to primitive peoples.

Yet minute as these monastic efforts at evangelisation may appear in relation to the millions of the population among which the monks settled, they had an immediate and a beneficial effect, and it seemed to many, even after the First World War, that monastic communities, which would in time become completely native in personnel, by their provision of a centre of liturgical worship within a larger community of social workers, teachers, nurses and agriculturists might perform on a small scale – and perhaps ulti-mately on a larger scale – something of the function of a Fulda or a St Gall in the christianising of Germany. It was not to be, at least not in our time and in the measure expected. Two world wars, the rapid spread of air travel and the media of mass communication and propaganda, the collapse of the Asian and African empires of the British, French, Dutch, German and Belgian peoples, and the sudden and wholly unforeseen fragmentation of Africa and parts of Asia into independent states with a bias against the religion and the emissaries of the old 'imperial' powers – all this profoundly changed the climate and outlook in all the less-developed countries. A few of the Benedictine and Cistercian communities remain, a few have been added since 1945 in the Cameroons and the Congo, only to be removed after a short stay by political disturbance. At the moment (1968) any prophecy as to the part monasticism may play as a civilising agency is wholly without value.

17 The Cistercians and Carthusians in the modern world

When peace returned to Europe after the Revolutionary and Napoleonic turmoil there was no Cistercian order in existence. The revival was at first sporadic. Pope Pius VII restored an abbey or two in the papal states, and here and there in Europe a new start was made, as in Belgium and France, but it was not till 1869, after almost a century of lapse, that a general chapter of the order met in Rome.

In the eighteenth century, the 'unreformed' section of the order was numerous in Germany and the Austrian empire. They had come to resemble the black monks in many respects. They taught schools and administered parishes in considerable numbers. Many of these abbeys were swept away, in part by the secular rulers, and later by the French conquerors, but a few lingered into the nineteenth century. On the other hand, the strict observance of the old model, almost entirely confined to France, ceased to exist at the Revolution. Alone, the small family of La Trappe survived by a series of strange happenings. A French monk, Dom Augustin de Lestrange, succeeded in collecting from the wreckage of the Revolution a group of his confrères and settling them in an abbey of his foundation, Valsainte in Switzerland. They were expelled in due course, but after innumerable difficulties, wanderings, new foundations and false starts, with harassments which included imprisonment and exile in America for Dom Lestrange, it was possible to rally a community and restore conventual life at the old site of La Trappe (1815). The heroic Dom Lestrange, however, had in the course of his wanderings added new austerities to the life which went even beyond those of Rancé, in the unjustified conviction that he was thus following the first fathers. This had caused the departure of a splinter-group that adhered to the discipline of the original founder of La Trappe. Subsequently the abbey of Westmalle became independent under political duress, and adopted with a more exactly historical purity the Charter of

Charity and early statutes. Dom Lestrange, after thirty years of devoted toil, remained with his followers alone at La Trappe with his version of the observance. Despite these disagreements, all four versions of Cistercian life, those of Lestrange, Rancé, Westmalle and the unreformed, were grouped together by the Roman administration and so remained till 1891. In the interval, however, tensions had been mounting. The Trappists, by their austerities which captured the imaginations both of the genuinely heroic and of the romantics, had become celebrated as the *ne plus ultra* of monastic devotion and had steadily increased in numbers as compared with the common observance. These, nevertheless, had continued to exist and had even increased their involvements in parochial and educational activities. At the same time, the fact that the Trappists were predominantly French, while the common observance was German-Austrian by nationality, embittered relations, especially after 1870. Finally in 1892 the three groups of Trappists were united to form an order entirely separate from the common observance. They gradually abandoned specifically Trappist (as opposed to primitive Cistercian) practices and ideals, and in 1902 they took the name of Cistercians of the strict observance (O.C.R.) as opposed to the Sacred Order of Cîteaux (S.O. Cist.).

The latter body, though bearing the brunt of two great wars and communist occupation, have grown steadily from 780 choir monks in 1894 to 1,170 in 1955. They have, in addition to abbeys in central Europe, a few houses in France and the Low Countries, and since 1925 have supported foundations in the USA and Vietnam. In contrast to this, the strict observance (still widely known as Trappists) had almost all their abbeys in France before the 1880s, when they were exiled by a hostile government and scattered in Holland, Spain and elsewhere. A single house in England, Mount St Bernard in Charnwood Forest, Leicestershire, was founded as early as 1835 by the enthusiastic convert, Ambrose Phillipps (de Lisle) with monks from Melleray in France. It remained something of a wonder (to the poet Wordsworth among others) and came near to extinction in the 1920s, but has subsequently doubled in numbers and buildings. Most of the monks exiled from France had returned before 1914, but there were losses of houses and personnel in both World Wars. Despite this, their numbers rose steadily from fifty-two houses with 2,900 monks in 1891, to fifty-eight with 3,700 in 1940 and seventy-two with 4,300 in 1960. By far the most spectacular advance was in north America, where the two abbeys existing in 1940, Gethsemany (Ky), the monastic home of Thomas Merton, and New Melleray (Iowa), gave birth to nine daughters with a total in 1967 of 700 professed monks and brothers, a number second only to France (976) among the nations of the world.

Their daily time-table may be given here, to be compared with those of Benedictine houses given on a later page. It is the horarium for weekdays in summer, reckoned by British summer time, of Mount St Bernard, Leicestershire.

    3.15 rise
    3.30 Vigils (also known as Nocturns or Matins)
          Private Masses
    5.30 mixt (a drink of coffee and crust of bread)
          reading
    6.50 Lauds – say 20 min.
          reading
    8.00 Conventual Mass – say 1 hr
          Terce $\frac{1}{4}$hr after Mass
          reading
   10.00 morning work begins
   12.00 morning work ends
   12.15 Sext, and short prayer
   12.30 dinner
          reading
    2.15 none

2.30	afternoon work begins
4.30	afternoon work ends
	reading
5.30	Vespers and $\frac{1}{4}$hr prayer
6.15	supper
	reading
7.15	Chapter
7.30	Compline, and short prayer
8.00	retire

In addition, each monk devotes at least one half hour to private mental prayer. There is no set 'recreation'; necessary conversations, spiritual or administrative, are permitted in times of 'reading', as are small private and domestic duties. Reading includes both directly spiritual reading, as also theology and study, letter-writing, and so on. As will have been seen, this time-table gives to the three component occupations of the rule of St Benedict – prayer, reading and work – a notional equality of four hours each, more or less. It follows the rule in giving an early retirement (before sunset in the midsummer months), with a fair allowance of sleep, and a very early rise for the night choirs.

The Carthusians at the epoch of the Reformation were at their maximum extension, with some two hundred houses scattered over almost every European country. Though their life was still as austere as ever, they had received many benefactions, and some of their monasteries, such as the Certosa at Pavia and that at Miraflores near Burgos, were elaborate and beautiful in architecture and decoration. After regional catastrophes in the seventeenth century, which included their disappearance in England and the heroic martyrdom of the London monks, there was another revival, particularly in France, Italy and Spain, and when once more the order had been beaten to the ground by the French Revolution there was a modest recovery in the nineteenth century. At present there are some twenty-five Charterhouses in the world, mostly in France and Italy; a few pioneers recently responded to invitations from the USA, but a regular Charterhouse has not yet established itself there. One of the largest houses is at Parkminster (Sussex, England), which was originally (1883) intended to house French monks then threatened with exile.

Pledged to a life of penance, solitude and prayer wholly apart from the world, without any concession to temporal interests and values, they are a standing witness to the unseen, and their vocation demands a very rare combination of spiritual, psychological and physical qualities. They receive many postulants, of whom few persevere, and whereas in the twelfth century many recruits came from other monastic and canonical orders, in the modern world there are more successful aspirants from the ranks of the secular clergy than from monastic homes. The image of the Charterhouse, never refaced because never defaced, remains the same as ever in the modern world, where it is the only hermit-order to have retained throughout its original medieval character.

7 *Cistercian foundations of the nineteenth and twentieth centuries* The grey lines show the foundations of the traditional 'unreformed' Cistercians (S. O. CIST.). This order is divided into Congregations (Meherau, Sénanque, Austria, St Bernard, Casamari, etc.) which are responsible for the foundations, shown as clearly as may be in a small map. The purple lines show the houses of the reformed Cistercians (Trappists, O.C.R.); these are made by individual houses, almost all in France, save

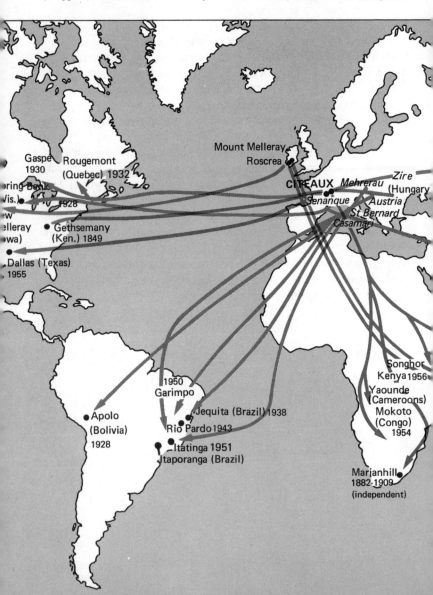

Gaspé
1930

Rougemont
(Quebec) 1932

ring Bank
Vis.)
1928

ew
elleray
wa)

Gethsemany
(Ken.) 1849

Dallas (Texas)
1955

Mount Melleray
Roscrea

CITEAUX   Mehrerau

Sénanque   Austria

St Bernard

Casamari

Zire
(Hungary

Songhor
Kenya 1956

Yaounde
(Cameroons)

Mokoto
(Congo)
1954

Apolo
(Bolivia)
1928

1950
Garimpo

Jequita (Brazil) 1938

Rio Pardo 1943

Itatinga 1951
Itaporanga (Brazil)

Marjanhill
1882-1909
(independent)

for the foundations from the two Irish houses, Mount Melleray and Roscrea.
In several cases it has been impossible on this scale to give the precise location.
Some of the houses in the Far East have been expelled or reduced to a minimum.
The foundations of the modern Benedictine congregations, described in the text,
were even more widespread, but the number of founding houses made graphic
representation impossible.

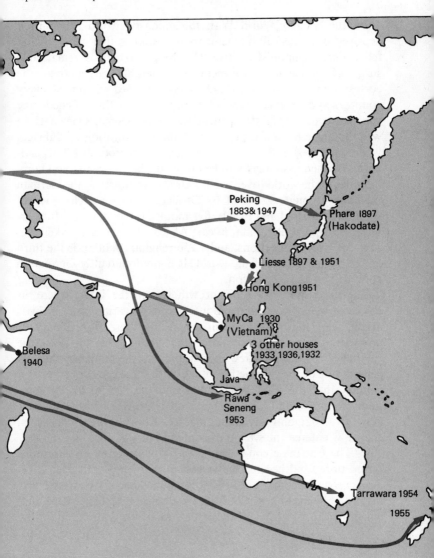

18 The present day

After the Second World War, the monastic world found itself deprived of almost all its members in countries that were, or that fell under, communist control. On the other hand a remarkable surge of monastic recruitment, considerably larger than the corresponding wave in 1919–25, was observed in almost every country, and in every type of observance. In three Benedictine spheres in particular the growth was phenomenal. One of these was the austere French province of the congregation of Subiaco, where the abbey of Pierre-qui-vire with its numerous direct dependencies on the mission grew to be one of the half-dozen largest communities in the world (over two hundred). Another was the German missionary congregation of St Ottilien. With an arch-abbey of some two hundred and twenty-five monks, three others – Munsterschwarzach, 320, Peramiko in east Africa 148, and Schweikelberg, 120 – of large proportions, and 1,256 religious in all, it is the third largest congregation of the world. It is predominantly German in composition and inspiration.

The third sphere of rapid growth was in the USA, where, as has been seen, two congregations, one of Bavarian, one of Swiss origin, were the only powerful groups. In these from the 1930s onwards, and particularly after the Second World War, the rhythm of recruitment grew more rapid and the monks of the new generations of the twentieth century, with a college education in a country that the First World War and the new media of communication had unified, and in a sense de-provincialised, showed a new spirit, outgoing, dynamic, mature. Always ardent educators, they now entered the stream of contemporary science and scholarship. The Cassinese congregation in particular grew to enormous proportions, and became the largest in the world with over 2,000 monks. The arch-abbey of St Vincent, with some 270 professed was surpassed by the abbey of St John the Baptist at Collegeville, Minn, which is at present by far the largest monastic community in the

St John's Abbey, Collegeville, Minnesota, founded 1856. The abbey church,
1953–61 (architects Marcel Breuer and Hamilton Smith), is an early example of
the revolution in church architecture after the Second World War. The windowless
block on the left is the chapterhouse with the monastery beyond. The low
building between bell-tower and west front is the baptistery.

world, with some 350 monks, though many of these are scattered in dependencies and mission stations. Besides its numbers Collegeville is distinguished by its strong educational and critical climate. It provides the staff of a university, and its buildings, partly the work of the architect Breuer and situated in a region of pine forests and lakes, provided one of the first examples in America of a new style of church architecture (now itself perhaps outmoded) which broke entirely with the conventional features of eastern sanctuary, cruciform plan and tower or spire, and produced a centrally placed altar years before Vatican ii, and a west end of striking modernity. The congregation has now nineteen monasteries, almost all of which have upwards of seventy professed religious. At the present time almost every state of the Union has some Benedictine activity within its bounds, whether abbey, priory, school, parish, mission station or chaplaincy, while St John's, Collegeville, in particular is also a focus of literary and scholarly work, and, in these latter days, of conferences and discussions of every kind.

19 Anglican monasteries

An account of modern monasticism would be incomplete without a glance at the communities of religious that have existed in the Anglican church during the past hundred years.[23] Quite apart from any consideration of the relationship of medieval religious to the Holy See – remote in the case of the monks, immediate in that of the friars, and part of the *raison d'être* of the later Jesuits – the Reformers of the sixteenth century, and Wyclif before them, were hostile towards any form of the religious life, partly because monasticism had no warranty in Scripture and the primitive church, partly because the vows of obedience and chastity were considered to be contrary to the spirit and liberty of a Christian and destructive of the conception of Christians as a family with one mind and intent. When, however, in the first half of the seventeenth century the higher levels of clergy and laity in England felt the attraction of the theological scholarship and devotional zeal of the Counter-Reformation, and the 'Anglo-Catholic' outlook appeared, it might have been thought that some form of religous life might make its appearance, especially as the Catholic recusant families were giving so many of their sons and daughters to monasteries and nunneries in France and the Low Countries. No doubt the contemporary and already traditional antipathy to monasticism, to which the Puritans gave violent expression, forbade the thought, though throughout the seventeenth century hopes were aired by devotional writers. The only experiment of the kind was the community of Little Gidding, where for almost twenty years (1626–46) two families of the relatives of Nicholas Ferrar (1592–1637) amounting to some thirty persons, lived an ordered life, part monastery, part imitation of an early Christian community, leaving a fragrant memory for contemporaries that clings still to the pages of Izaak Walton, and of John Shorthouse's novel, *John Inglesant*, and (so visitors claim) to the church of Little Gidding today. It was almost exactly two centuries before the next attempt at a quasi-monastic community was made by John Henry Newman at Littlemore, near Oxford, in 1842. Thenceforward, among those influenced by the Oxford movement, there was a steady, if not large, stream of foundations, some of men, the majority of women, which has continued to the present day. Forty years ago Coulton could write that the numbers of Anglican nuns in England exceeded the number of Catholic nuns in the middle ages. Institutes of men, with which alone we are concerned, were fewer. Mortality was high among them, as might be expected in a way of life which was not officially sponsored by the Church of England and only achieved rights of citizenship by degrees. Of the thirty-four 'orders and societies' that have been listed as existing between 1842 and 1961, five ultimately joined the Roman Catholic church and nineteen became extinct, leaving only ten survivors. We may confine our attention to four of these, the only ones to have retained corporate existence for more than half a century: those of Cowley, Mirfield, Kelham and Nashdom.

The Society of St John the Baptist had its origin in 1865 among a small group which included Mr Charles Wood, later second Viscount Halifax, and the Rev. R. M. Benson, then vicar of Cowley, already a suburb of Oxford, but not yet the industrial partner of the city. Edward Bouverie Pusey supported the venture. Benson, a Tractarian, was a very remarkable man, energetic, ascetic, apostolic, no Anglo-Catholic and no lover of aesthetic or liturgical elaboration, but with a saintly and therefore compelling personality. The object of the Society was 'to seek that sanctification to which God in His Mercy calls us, and in so doing to seek, as far as God may permit, to be instrumental in bringing others to be partakers of the same sanctification' – a somewhat wordy, but admirable expression of an outgoing religious life. The horarium of Cowley may be given; like most of the Anglican institutes, it follows in essentials the classical outline:

5.15 rise
5.45 Matins, Lauds and Prime
7.00 Mass
8.00 breakfast
9.00 Meditation – at least one hour's mental prayer
      is made during the day
10.00 Terce, followed by study
12.45 Sext
 1.00 dinner and recreation in common
 2.00 none
      exercise – a walk
 6.45 supper
 9.15 Compline

Besides providing a focus of spiritual and liturgical life in Oxford, and a considerable literary output, the Cowley Fathers have always been in demand as preachers, directors, conductors of retreats and counsellors of nuns. They have founded congregations in the USA and Canada, and have engaged in missionary enterprises in India and Africa, while the American congregation has a province in Japan.

The community of the Resurrection, known sometimes (incorrectly) as 'Mirfield monks', owed its existence to the social conscience of a group of clergy of whom the outstanding member was Charles Gore, and the first community, including Gore himself and Walter Frere, made their profession at Pusey House, Oxford, in 1892. Their purpose, in Gore's words, was 'to devote our lives to prayer, study and work'. From early times, under the influence of Gore, the life was less monastic than that of Cowley, with simple austerity, a liberty of opinion and a democracy of government. The life-long vows were taken to a rule rather than to a superior. The first 'Senior' was Gore, and the community under his guidance moved from Pusey House to Radley, and thence to

Westminster and Mirfield, a mansion built by a wealthy mill-owner in a valley near Huddersfield (Yorks). In the year of this move (1898) Gore became bishop of Worcester and was succeeded as superior by Walter Frere, who was appointed bishop of Truro in 1922. The aim of the life at Mirfield was to reproduce that of the early Christians. Thus, whether consciously or not, Gore had as his ideal the *apostolica vita*, the life of the first Christians in Jerusalem that had inspired so many religious orders in the twelfth century, and had led ultimately to the birth of the Dominican friars.

The Mirfield community, besides guiding their noviciate and meeting calls to preach and give retreats, manage an adjoining retreat-house and a training college for ordinands. Since 1903 they have actively engaged in missionary and teaching work in South Africa and Rhodesia (Bishop Huddleston is a member of their body) and from the beginning of the century have been prominent in all kinds of contacts with the Roman Catholic church (as at the Malines conferences), the Orthodox and the Scandinavian churches. Besides Gore and Frere several other members of the community have become bishops in the United Kingdom and Commonwealth.

The Society of the Sacred Mission, founded in London in 1894 to train lay workers for the foreign missions, settled at Kelham (Notts) in 1903, and became a training college for ordinands at home and abroad. The members of the community 'vow themselves to the divine service under the conditions of Poverty, Chastity and Obedience', with the threefold aim of increasing the number of those who give themselves to the divine service, of labouring for the conversion and perfection of souls, especially among the heathen and abroad, and of cultivating divine service (i.e. liturgical prayer). The Society is thus among the 'active' orders, but their emphasis upon an austere life, with the Day Hours, a 'dialogue' community Mass, Mattins and choral Evensong makes them comparable to the Benedictine congregation of St Ottilien.

The three Anglican 'orders' hitherto mentioned have several characteristics in common. In the first place they rest upon the traditional pillars of the religious life (which the early reformers uprooted), with permanent vows of chastity, poverty (with certain restrictions) and community life under obedience. Next, they adopt in whole or in part the monastic version of the divine office and the Roman missal, and the *Opus Dei* is performed with dignity in a setting of beauty. In this again they are traditional. Thirdly, they have all been deeply concerned with missionary and social work overseas, particularly in countries that until 1945 were members of the British Empire (or Commonwealth). How far the dissolution of the Commonwealth has limited and will still further limit the scope of their work is not yet fully clear. Finally, there is in all three of these bodies a strongly English, vernacular, wholesome and bracing ingredient, an avoidance of extravagance, romance, antiquarianism and aestheticism.

Contrary to the vague opinion of many, the number of 'monks' in the Church of England is small. The spectacular vagaries of Father Ignatius of Llanthony and elsewhere, and the widespread *réclame* created for his abbey by the first abbot of Caldey, both before and after the 'conversion' of the community in 1913, added to the unsuccessful attempts of individuals to establish monastic groups here and there, have established in many minds the image of numerous monastic bodies of varying degrees of eccentricity. In fact, there is only a single monastic body that has been in existence for anything approaching fifty years' space. This is Nashdom Abbey, Burnham, Bucks, which in its present state is a staid and retiring establishment. The community derives from Caldey through Dom Anselm Mardon, the only solemnly professed monk of Caldey who in 1913 remained in the Anglican communion. He established himself with one or two ex-Caldey brothers at Pershore, with the Rev. Denys Prideaux, an oblate of Caldey in holy orders, as chaplain. When Dom Mardon himself left to join the Roman Catholic church Father Denys, after the difficult years of the First World War, was induced to make his profession and become abbot. He was a scholar of parts, and gradually gave to his community a spirit different from that of Caldey. Caldey, apart from its abbot, was Cistercian rather than Benedictine in spirit; few of its members had had a university education. Abbot Prideaux favoured the traditional Benedictine life of the liturgy, richly performed in ample buildings, and an emphasis on learned work. In 1926 he purchased Nashdom, a magnificent creation of Lutyens for a Russian client, and gradually built up a monastic life that satisfied his ideal. His successors have continued his work and a community of forty now conducts a solemn performance of the liturgy according to the Roman monastic rite, following a time-table similar to that of the typical continental Benedictine house of today. House and garden work are done by the monks, many of whom devote themselves to study or writing, while others preach, give retreats and minister to the needs of their neighbours, spiritual and physical. There is a constant succession of guests, clerical and lay, who come for retreats and spiritual counsel. Whereas Caldey in its Anglican days, partly in self-defence, adopted the historically indefensible position that Benedictine abbeys in the early middle ages were extra-diocesan and outside episcopal control, Nashdom has assumed and accepted a place in Anglican life under the patronage of bishops. One of their number, Dom Bernard Clements, was given the Vicarage of All Saints, Margaret Street, London, by the bishop of London, and Gregory Dix, Benedict Frost and Anselm Hughes have made reputations in the fields of liturgiology, mystical theology and musicology. Nevertheless, to an outsider it seems a plant of a more exotic character than, say, Cowley or Mirfield. Though these very naturally make use of ancient and more modern

Catholic spirituality, the end-product of their teaching is essentially English, Anglican, non-Roman. Nashdom, on the contrary, is a Benedictine abbey, akin (at least to the casual observer) in life, liturgy and spirituality to a hundred others, and though sincerely rooted in the Anglican church it is not those roots that nourish its flower and fruit.

20 Daily life of the monk

No account of western monasticism would be complete without a description of the daily life as lived by monks. It does not require much imagination to realise that this is not an easy task. A horarium is a basic essential, but how little does this tell us of the life as lived by the individual. It is only when we have personal accounts of the human incidents and spiritual experiences within a monastery that we begin to understand, and how rare these are in comparison to the number of communities in existence at any single moment of time. What would the horarium of Rievaulx in 1160 or of St Joseph's, Avila, in 1565 tell us of the life in a community where Ailred was abbot or Teresa prioress? It is only when we read the writings of Ailred or the *Life of Ailred* by his disciple Walter Daniel, or the autobiography of St Teresa and the vivid sketches of her nuns in her *Foundations* that we begin to see the experience of one who lived within the framework of a time-table.

With medieval monasticism there are two further 'technical' difficulties. The one is that exact times are rarely given, while indications such as sunrise and sunset, dawn, dusk and 'about midnight' are common. Even when an exact hour is named, the reckoning (at least in the greater part of the middle ages) is by the ancient system of twelve day and night hours varying in length according to the season's ration of light and darkness. The second difficulty is that the daily horarium, including even the time and number of meals, varies with the season (winter and summer) and with the liturgical character of the day (feast day, ordinary day, fast day). All that we can do in this brief study is to select a particular season to represent all the year. We will consider first, the horarium of St Benedict's monastery in AD 540, then an English abbey just after the Norman Conquest (*c*. 1075), and finally a modern Benedictine house.[27]

At Monte Cassino in St Benedict's day the following would seem to have been the skeleton time-table on 1 November; no allowance is made for the more recent festival of All Saints:

2.00 a.m.   rise for nocturns (the modern Matins)
2.10–3.30   nocturns
3.30–5.00   reading
5.00–5.45   Lauds
5.45–8.15   reading, including Prime (twenty minutes)
8.15–2.30   work, broken by Terce, Sext and None (10 mins each)
2.30–3.15   dinner
3.15–4.15   reading
4.15–4.45   Vespers, collation (reading), Compline
5.15   in bed by this time

In summer, say 30 June, the time-table would have been:

 1.00– 2.00   nocturns
 2.15– 3.00   Lauds
 3.00– 4.30   reading
 4.30– 9.15   Prime and work
 9.30–11.30   reading
11.45–12.30   dinner
12.30– 2.00   siesta
 2.00– 6.30   work
 6.30– 7.00   Vespers
 7.00– 7.30   supper and collation
 7.30– 8.00   compline and bed.

In both these time-tables the waking day, apart from meals, is divided roughly into Office (*Opus Dei*), reading, and work, to which respectively four, four and five to six hours are devoted.

To the modern mind the most surprising feature of this horarium is the nocturnal activity. To rise at 2 a.m. on a winter morning and, after an hour's psalmody, spend more than three hours (interrupted by more psalmody) in reading or writing would seem preposterous, especially when the ineffective lamps or candles of the age enter into the picture. Perhaps to St Benedict and his world our own convention would seem equally absurd, that in the six months

Bee-keeping at Monte Cassino.
From a ninth-century manuscript
in the Vatican Library.

April to September we should spend from two to five hours asleep while the world is bathed in sunshine and then at the day's end re-create ourselves or complete our work by artificial light for five hours or so. In other words, granted that sleep is restricted to seven or eight hours in duration, many hours of the waking day, in all save about three of the summer months, must be passed in artificial light. There is plenty of evidence that at least until the fourteenth century all busy men, as well as labourers, began their day from 5 a.m. onwards. St Benedict, it is clear, regarded nightfall as the ruling moment. When darkness fell, and in central Italy this would be about 5 p.m. at the winter solstice and 7.45 at mid-summer, the day ended, and from that moment the rest of the horarium was calculated. A consequence of this was the necessity of filling in the early hours of the day. We may remind ourselves that the agricultural population in Europe, until very recent times, rose at sunrise or before, and in the summer compensated for the short night with a siesta of two hours. We may also remember that even today in Mediterranean lands the night, particularly in the lighter half of the year, sees very much more general activity than in northern latitudes. Local trains run throughout the night and are well filled. The foolish virgins of the parable anticipated no difficulty in buying oil at midnight, and they would probably be able to do so in a town of Calabria or Crete today.

The second source of surprise may be the apparently unbroken round of duties. Here, however, we are allowing ourselves to be deceived by the form of the document behind our time-table. The rule of St Benedict does not include a horarium; the horarium is deduced from what it tells us, and in any case a horarium is never a complete picture of a community's life. While it is probably true that set periods of recreation – seated conversation, private reading, strolling round the garden, games of one sort or another – such as occur in the day's round of most modern religious houses, were

not allowed for in early monasticism, it is clear that in any community endless duties and necessities for conversation would exist which do not appear in the time-table – obtaining clothes, boots and tools, receiving practical instructions, spiritual advice or medical care, all the hundred and one tasks and needs that would occur in a small community housed in a relatively small building. As for the long periods of reading, St Benedict himself makes allowance for those who cannot or will not read, and who therefore must be employed in other work, and reading would have included the

preparation of liturgical duties, writing and teaching. We may remember that the community envisaged by St Benedict contained few priests or clerics, and that it was under very close surveillance from the abbot, who would himself arrange the day's work and encourage, advise and correct at all times. The work itself would be of all kinds – field, garden, vine and olive culture, crafts, repairs, the care of beasts. Possibly also the more material preparations for writing and teaching were made in worktime. The life described was an austere life, but it was also a healthy life and one full of physical activity; it was not a life that would impose severe psychological strains or lead to introversion or neurosis, and for those with a true vocation for it there would be abundant opportunity for both the warmth of mutual assistance and the silence of private prayer.

More than five centuries later we can see the horarium of an English monastery, the largest in the country, Christ Church, Canterbury. The winter scheme was as follows:

2.30		rise
		prayers with seven psalms
		psalms 119–150
		Nocturns
		several more psalms for the royal house
		Matins and Lauds of the Dead
		Matins of All Saints
5.00–	6.00	reading
6.00–	6.45	Lauds
		psalm *miserere*
		psalms and prayers for royal house
		anthems
6.45		Prime
		seven penitential psalms
		litany of the saints

7.30–	8.00	reading
8.00–		seven psalms
		Terce
		psalms for royal house
		Chapter or Morrow Mass
		meeting in chapter-house, followed by psalms for dead
9.45–12.00		work
12.00		Sext
		psalms and prayers for relatives, etc.
		High Mass
1.30		None
		psalms and prayers for relatives etc.
2.00		Dinner
2.45–	4.30	reading or work
4.30		Vespers
		psalms for relatives,
		anthems
		Vespers of All Saints
		Vespers of Dead
5.30		reading
6.15		Compline
		psalm *miserere*
		five psalms
6.30		retire

In addition, there were processions before the High Mass three days
a week and some extra prayers omitted from the list above.

The contrast between St Benedict's horarium and this, which is
that drawn up by Lanfranc, is very great. Of the time, roughly
fourteen hours, available after the hours of sleep, meals and toilet
have been deducted, no less than eight are occupied in religious
services in church, while reading has less than three hours and
work three at most. Moreover the liturgical duties were, for the
ordinary member of the community, intangible. All remaining

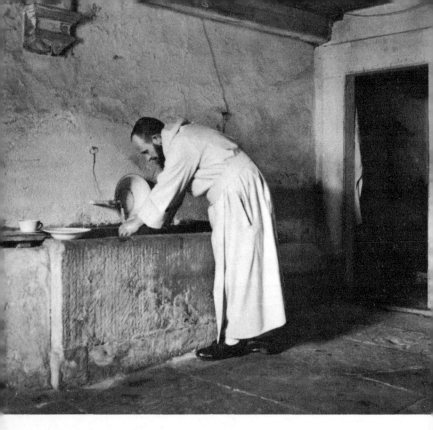

occupations, small and great, and any moment of rest and quiet, came out of the reading or work, as did any giving of instruction, counsel, and so forth, and even perhaps a priest's private Mass. Add to this that after the long periods of standing and chanting many must have been physically and psychologically exhausted, and in need of some kind of rest before settling down to work of any kind. What, we may ask, had made the change? Above all, two weighty additions. The first was the two Masses daily attended by the whole community – perhaps three, if the priest's private Mass was taken out of reading or work time. The second was the large quantity of psalms, prayers, litanies and minor offices. Besides these, both office and Mass had been lengthened by the chant, which was now far more elaborate than in St Benedict's day. The result was to make the monastic life something very different. While the life of the rule was a busy, balanced life, with plenty of physical movement and hours in the open air, that of the Cluniac monachism and of the English customs (both derived ultimately from the practice of Carolingian days) was an indoor, sedentary life in which there was little physical movement and exertion, but more psychological and physiological weariness. It was a fully liturgical life, with the greater part of the day spent in the choir, and with an accent on vocal prayer and public intercession. Looked at from another angle, the monastic life had changed from what was in essence that of a small family, serving God in prayer and mutual encouragement in a life that was primarily ascetic in the widest sense of that word – a progress in virtue and charity with the aid of obedience and the abbot's counsel and command – to one that was primarily the solemn service of God and intercession for the king and other members of society. The contrast must not be exaggerated. Manuscripts, illumination and original literary work, the advancement of many monks to successful and fruitful careers as bishops, show that time could be found for work of high quality and that the liturgical life did not crush personal and pastoral ability. Saints were nurtured at Winchester and Canterbury as they had been in the simpler life of Monte Cassino and Jarrow. Nevertheless, the contrast is there, and it serves to explain the form taken by the Cistercian revolution, which by shearing off almost all the liturgical accretions save for the Mass, and by simplifying the chant and ceremonial, restored work and reading and private prayer to their earlier position as partners of the *Opus Dei*.

For the observance of today it is not possible to find a time-table that is common to all. Moreover, in the case of the congregations occupied in teaching or apostolic work, the official horarium bears little relation to the actual day's work of the majority of the community, who may be occupied for the greater part of the day in tasks which could not figure on any formal time-table. Instead, we may take the official horarium of the congregation of France, which is the largest and most widely diffused of those groups who make the liturgical service the central feature of their life and who, as communities, are as uniform in their daily occupations as can be expected of a group of men in a large monastery. The time-table, here as elsewhere nowadays, is basically the same throughout the year, save for Holy Week, Christmas, and a few other feast days.

5.00	rise
5.30	Matins and Lauds ($\frac{3}{4}$ hour to $1\frac{1}{4}$ hours)
	Private Masses ($\frac{1}{2}$ hour) and prayer
8.15	Prime.
	Breakfast taken standing before or after Prime coffee and roll
	spiritual reading
10.00	Terce and High Mass
11.00–12.50	work, chiefly study, writing or administration
12.50	Sext
1.00	dinner, followed by recreation in common
2.30	none, followed by manual work indoors or out
4.30	Vespers
5.00– 7.00	work – for most, this is study
7.00	twice a week, conference from the abbot, choir practice, etc.
7.30	supper, followed by free time
8.30	Compline
	retire

In addition to these duties, private prayer (i.e. 'mental prayer') of half-an-hour is an obligation to be fitted in as best suits the individual, and there are occasional, but not daily, short services such as Benediction of the Blessed Sacrament.

It will be seen that this is a long way towards being a return to the time-table of St Benedict's rule. The great addition is the Mass. Until recently, besides the high (or conventual) Mass, all priests said a private Mass also. Now, there is concelebration at the High

Mass and only a few say private Masses as well as attending the High Mass. Taken altogether public and private prayer occupy four to four and a half hours, spiritual reading at least one hour, and manual work at least one and a half hours, with four other hours shared in different quantities by different individuals between spiritual reading, study and manual work. Conversation or 'free time', not specifically allowed for by St Benedict or early medieval customs, is universal in modern monasteries and on Sundays and other specified days is prolonged and allows for a walk of some distance. There is also considerable difference, even in the congregations engaged in 'active' works, between the customs of nationalities. Thus English and American monasteries make greater allowance for physical exercise than most of the continental congregations. The Solesmes horarium is indeed perhaps nearer than any other to the central tradition of Benedictine life carried over from the middle ages into the Vannist and Maurist congregations.

21 The monastic life: a reappraisal

Ten or a dozen years ago a survey of the monastic life in the modern world could have ended on a note of quiet satisfaction. All over the free world where monks existed there seemed to be an increase rather than a slackening of recruitment, and the monastic vocation appeared as one that appealed to the sorely tired minds of today, while in every department of monastic activity, whether scholarly, educational or missionary, solid work was being done for the needs of the church. More recently, however, in the past four or five years, a sudden and unforeseen change has come about. The absolute coincidence in time seems to lead inevitably to the conclusion that this change is due to the same hidden causes that lay behind the summoning, the deliberations and decisions of the Second Vatican Council. There, and throughout the church, there has been a profound movement of sentiment and a strange division of mind. On the one hand, there has been the enthusiasm of forces released from bondage and springing forward to action, and on the other a profound malaise and questioning. Nowhere is this more apparent than in the monastic sector of the church's life, where, for the moment at least, there is a keen sense of landmarks lost and of low visibility on the road ahead.

The horrors of war, oppression and violence, the loosening of so many moorings in the realms of science, psychology and ethics, the kaleidoscope of dissolving empires and mushroom nations, the mingled opportunities and frustrations of the new world are undoubtedly among the springs and impulses behind the yearning for some new security and goal of enterprise and the fatigue in listening to the praise of past times. Rarely indeed has the monastic body been free from inner tensions. The rhythm of decline and renewal and the stresses of reformers and conservatives are endemic in monastic history. But normally the struggle has been between laxity and zeal, between mediocrity and observance, and the end to be attained has been clear – the better observance of whatever interpretation of the rule and of evangelical perfection in this way or in that seemed acceptable. There was a general agreement as to the ideal, however near or far the target of performance might be set. Today, however, the anxiety goes deeper. Throughout the monastic body, as throughout the church, positions and ideals hitherto regarded as intangible are being questioned. Priestly celibacy, physical penances and austerities, the traditional liturgy, retirement from 'the world', even the permanent monastic vows and the concepts of obedience and humility are being canvassed, and the atmosphere is charged with criticism and experiment. There has been a distressing exodus of individuals of all ages from almost every order. Meanwhile all religious orders are experiencing a shortage of recruits which is without recent parallel as a universal phenomenon outside times of war, and which is perhaps in part cause and in part an effect of the prevailing malaise.

The liturgical movement, which began some sixty years ago with the aim of purifying from the accretions of the past five centuries the Missal, Gradual and monastic antiphoner, with their chant, and of substituting the Mass and divine office of the medieval golden age for the extra-liturgical prayers and devotions that had multiplied, has rapidly and recently become an endeavour to reproduce in contemporary formulas the Eucharistic liturgy and the Christian faithful of the early centuries. This has had an unexpected backlash. Just as, in the eleventh and twelfth centuries there was a steady 'monachisation' of the canonical bodies, of the clergy, and of the devout layfolk, so now there has been a practical 'de-monachisation' of the liturgy and the devotional life, in which the monks themselves have shared, not only in so far as the liturgical changes have been established by Rome and by the Council, but also by their own initiative in welcoming and extending the changes. Thus many monasteries accepted the considerable abbreviations of the divine office which were primarily intended to relieve the burden

laid upon the secular clergy, and more recently still there have been drastic curtailments and a flight from Latin. Similarly the monastic orders have accepted the many small physical easements that have been made for the church at large, such as the abolition of the Eucharistic fast and, in certain regions, the total cessation of the obligation of abstinence as well as that of fasting. Even such apparently neutral changes as the permission for afternoon and evening Mass, and concelebration, have tended to disrupt traditional time-tables and to shorten or render more physically easy the day's duties.

All this, necessary and welcome for the layfolk who form the great mass of the faithful as an *aggiornamento* that has adapted old worship to new conditions and activities and ways of thought, may nevertheless bring to the monastic life a physical and spiritual relaxation. If, in the middle ages, there was a tendency to regard the

Disciples of Athonias's School
on Mount Athos at grace before dinner,
wearing the characteristic headgear
of Orthodox ecclesiastics.

227

vowed monastic life as the only true and safe Christian life, now,
by a swing back of the pendulum, there is something of a flight
from any severity of discipline or observance.

Yet the life of evangelical perfection, aided and deepened by the
Holy Eucharist, is an essential part of the Christian message, and
is in its essence intangible and unchangeable, and the monastic life,
as seen in a tradition reaching back almost to the beginnings of
Christianity, is a canonised form of that life. There could, indeed,
be a church without monastic rules and religious orders, which are
in their details man-made, whereas there could not be a church
without the priesthood which was ordained by Christ to minister
his word and his sacraments to men; but the goal for which the
monastic life exists, as a visible framework and guiding-line to the
perfect following of Christ, will always exist, for the union of man's
will with that of God, in love and adoration, is the end of man's
creation.

What, then, shall we say is of the essence of monasticism, as a
way of life, that must be present now and in the future in any
scheme of that life? What does monasticism add to specify the
general way of life of all Christians? This question brings us face to
face with the problem which we avoided at the beginning of this
book, that is, the denial by many at various moments of history,
and not least at the present moment, of the validity of any distinction in the Christian church between what are commonly called
the lives of the commands and of the counsels, between those who
aim, as must all who believe in a divine revelation to mankind
through Jesus Christ, at observing all that Christ himself accepted
from the Old Law and proposed as his own enlargement in the New
Testament, and those who aim beyond this at fulfilling what Scripture and tradition present as his counsels, particularly in the two
great areas of personal relationship and personal ownership, commonly distinguished by the free undertaking of personal chastity

and the abandonment of the rights of possessing property. Let it be said at once that this distinction between counsel and command is a useful and perhaps unavoidable shorthand; but it is no more than that. In the Old Law and the New there is only one command, that of loving God with all the faculties and powers of man. To this all are called, and since the God of human beings cannot and has not commanded his children to commit race suicide or forbidden them to make good use of the world in which they have been created, he has not made the renunciation of marriage and of all possessions a condition of his service. He has, however, made the demand, and thereby offered to bestow the gift, of total love. He has also, in the Christian life, the life of grace, as in all forms of life, willed that, either by the working out of the forces of nature or by his own direct free choice, there should be difference of capacity and of gifts between his creatures in every kind of activity. And although God does not destroy by his commands what he has created in his goodness he does, by his revelation and by his call to union with himself, require, and invite, all who hear his call to aim higher, to look higher, than a purely human level. Christians, all Christians, are called to love others not less, but more, than if they were not Christians, but love is an equivocal word, even when used in the sense strictly defined by moralists and theologians, and in a Christian context it is the love of God as Father, of Christ as Saviour, and of others in God. How this love is best attained by the individual is life's problem and happiness for each. In every human life the choice has to be made between worthy and unworthy, greater and less noble love; for Christians there must always be the choice between things seen and things unseen, and every Christian is required, is called and is enabled to live a life essentially more spiritual than is merely human. All Christians are called to be chaste, to set their hearts on unseen, not on material wealth, and to obey God, not man. No creature in its essence is evil; but no creature, no human being, is God. Christ called to love; he also called to renunciation. He called to the heights; in his mercy he stooped to the ground; he called many, but said that few obeyed the call and were chosen. It is in this mystery that surrounds all the ultimates of human life, grace and freewill, predestination and justice, renunciation and fulfilment, that the Christian vocation and the monastic vocation must be left. Those who deny the foundations of those vocations must ask themselves, if they are Christians, whether any Christian life can be a purely natural, human life. There were those in the so-called ages of faith who would have had the whole world to be a monastery. In more modern times there have been those who deny the monastic life to be Christian. Neither of the two parties has seen to what results such opinions lead.

The monastic life is therefore, in the first place, an explicit and visible assertion of a way (not the only way) of moving towards a total acceptance of Christ's call, and as this requires a more than ordinary disentanglement from the attractions, distractions, desires and cares of 'the world' in the scriptural sense of merely earthly considerations, the element of withdrawal and solitude is essential. Moreover, to avoid loss of time and waste of effort, and to lessen the danger of ignorance and self-deceit, a rule of life and a qualified teacher are necessary. St Benedict saw the monastic life as others have seen the Christian life, as a warfare: 'Soldiering under a rule and an abbot', and this must be, normally, a lifelong service, and a lifelong service with others, who in a special way, as brothers of a single family, are the 'neighbours' towards whom the second commandment is directed. Within that life and family there must be a regime of diet and occupation that is simple and moderate in itself, giving opportunity and indeed occasion for self-denial and renouncement, and at the present day in countries of the western world in particular this needs reassertion as perhaps never before. A part of that regime will be set hours of prayer, both in common and in private. Here again the balance must be kept. Set, vocal, prayer in the form of the Office and liturgical prayer has, above its own efficacy, its strength and worth as the prayer of the whole community joined to the prayer of the whole church. Private prayer on the other hand must always be a mainspring of spiritual life; it is, of all moments, the meeting-place with God. For all this, a rule, approved by both authority and the experience of good men, is a necessary safeguard, and this rule must be observed, not with antiquarian or pharisaical precision, but with a faithfulness that maintains its character as an instrument of perfection. If the rule is kept faithfully, in the spirit in which it was composed, all will be well; if it is not kept, individuals may fare well, but the security of a firm standard has gone.

What has been said thus far might be true of any form of the regular life. What does the monastic profession demand beyond this? Here is where the point of decision comes, at the present day as in every other age. We must remember that in the specialisation and fragmentation of monastic life during the ages the limits have become very wide. A country may be converted to Christianity by individual priests working under a bishop, or by an order such as the White Fathers, dedicated to the mission, or by friars such as the Dominicans, or, finally, by a body of monks working partly by their activity in teaching and preaching to those around them, and partly by their presence as a Christian family. Similarly, among those who follow a monastic rule there may be a very great variety of employment, from the withdrawn austerity of a monastery of Trappists to the outgoing energy of an African house of monks of St Ottilien. In either case, if the rule is obeyed and the common life of frugality and prayer is maintained, the monastic life may be secure. But there is a limit, both in the declension from the life of evangelical, spiritually bracing austerity and in the outgoing, external employment of the community, beyond which any extension is not compatible with the essential requirements of the life. Living out of the monastery or out of its round of observance and service may be thought to transgress that limit. In the later chapters of this book we have seen that several congregations of both Benedictine and Cistercian monks since the Reformation have manned parishes, even in regions where the regular hierarchy of the church has been established. It will be found in almost all these cases that either the institute itself (as that of St Ottilien) was primarily 'active' in character, and adopted the monastic life only so far as was compatible with this, or that (as in the case of the English congregation) a specific Papal permission or privilege made allowances for special circumstances. In such cases we may say that a privilege or a dispensation itself establishes the existence of a general rule which it suspends. In the last resort it is not the name but the manner of life, that makes the monk, and unless we are to equate the monastic life with the religious life (of which it is now only a species) we must mark the line of division.

It may indeed be said that the monastic rule, and the life of a monk regulated by it, is in the nature of an education, a spiritual formation, which gives a man a norm of conduct for life and a particular spiritual depth to any subsequent employment. There is some truth in this, and it is undeniable that a priest with monastic experience, who has been faithful to all the demands of a parish life to which he has been sent, may achieve holiness of life that has in it a monastic character. The history of the church is full of examples of monastic bishops who have combined pastoral zeal with monastic virtue. One of the few modern Benedictines whose cause for beatification is active was an archbishop of Palermo of the nineteenth century. This, however, is no more than saying that neither monkhood nor priesthood, neither a solitary life nor an active one is of itself a guarantee of, or a bar to, holiness of life. What we are debating is not this, but a different question, whether there is a particular external framework of life that can be called monastic. The answer must surely be, Yes. What, then, is it?

Fifty years ago the term 'contemplative' would probably have been bandied about in such a discussion. At the moment the contemplative life is at a discount among those discussing the implications of the Second Vatican Council, and it is in any case a dangerous, ambiguous word, which changes its meaning and application as one shifts from the spiritual life of the individual to the external occupation of the community. In the latter realm, where its traditional sense is of engagement in occupations directed to no other end than the knowledge by the individual of the nature of God and his service, the number of modern monastic bodies who are strictly 'contemplative' is very small. The Camaldolese, the Carthusians, and in a looser sense, the Reformed Cistercians, would qualify for inclusion. But if we broaden the meaning of the word to include liturgical service and study Cluny, Bec and many fervent medieval houses might be admitted. Few modern Benedictine abbeys would qualify. With women, on the other hand, the number is far greater, and here, with such bodies as the Carmelites and the Poor Clares, the two senses of contemplative, external and spiritual, come near to merging. There must certainly, in any monastic life, be a contemplative element (using the word in its non-technical sense), that is, private prayer and meditative reading of the Bible and spiritual writers for no purpose save that of the spiritual life must be a notable part of any monastic time-table, but at other times of the day study in wider fields, or agricultural work with care and skill, may well be an employment, and, within certain fixed limits, teaching theology and preaching spiritual retreats.

The monastic community should be of a size to make the regular life with its full liturgical observance possible, while at the same time not so large as to make it impossible for an abbot to be the real father of his monks, watching over the welfare both of their human personality and (still more earnestly) of their soul in the day-to-day life of the monastery. It is not his business to be a preacher in great demand up and down the land, still less to be a familiar figure on television or at conferences. In an observant and fervent abbey a monk's life should be spent within the orbit of regular monastic life, and he should be both willing and psychologically able thus to remain for his lifetime. Herein lies the spiritual, true virtue of the vow of stability. The monk who cannot live without the prospect of change, variety, movement or holiday lacks a principal spiritual qualification for a monastic life.

Within the monastery the occupation taking precedence of all else should be the liturgical service of God, in the Divine Office and the Eucharist, and by and large all should attend all of this. In the community the common life should be observed absolutely. This does not imply universal and perpetual uniformity, but does imply a simplicity of life and an entire absence of privileges and proprietorship. All work or employment should ideally take place within the monastic precinct, for only so will the withdrawal be possible that is an essential feature of a monk's life; it is this solitude that gives him his name.

What a monk's work should be has been the great problem of monastic reformers from the late middle ages, and remains one at the present day. From the days of Cassiodorus till the early thirteenth century the principal employment of those in the community who had no administrative duties was the copying and illuminating of manuscripts and the drawing up of all documents needed in administration and litigation. It was an excellent 'background' employment, a task at once necessary, endless, varied, skilful, valuable. As all monks were literate save the small class of 'lay-brothers' in black monk houses and the larger class of converses in Cistercian abbeys, work could be found for all, from the clumsy beginner to the gifted artist, and the copyist would often become an author. This employment it was that from the age of Charlemagne onwards preserved the Latin and patristic classics and wove ancient learning into the texture of vernacular speech, and it was in the scriptoria of Frankland, of Germany and of England that the masterpieces of design and colour were produced – as earlier still in the cells of Ireland and Northumbria – that astonish us today when we turn from a reproduction to the original manuscript.

The disappearance of the manuscript implied the end of a pursuit that had occupied monastic cloisters for almost a millennium. No substitute of universal viability has been found. Printing would not do, for it was commercialised from the start, and demanded something of the business acumen mingled with knowledge and tact in human relations that are required in a modern publisher. The congregation of Sta Giustina was the first to give an impulse to study and literary work as a major occupation, and a century later the great developments in education took many monasteries into that field also, in imitation of (or in competition with) the Jesuits and secular clerics. Henceforward these two pursuits, singly or in combination, were to be the standard occupations. The Vannists and Maurists carried the organisation of learned work to perfection, and with all its ancillary demands and skills, including the copying of archival material, it sufficed for large numbers. For others, there were missions to neglected parishes and simple teaching. In other circles, as in Germany and among the English exiles, education at a secondary level was more commonly practised.

Neither of these was a perfect answer, for each demanded a high level of particular forms of mental ability, and each tended to take the monks out of the monastery, either to search for materials and books in archives or libraries, or to teach secular subjects in the class-room. Still less compatible with regular monastic life was the practice, in regions wasted or lost to the Catholic church by the wars of religion or lack of clergy, of monks serving parishes and even of residing in them, or, as with the English monks, of monks passing to the mission field among a hostile population.

In the revival of the nineteenth century the new congregations, especially those of Solesmes and Beuron, made of study and scholarship a principal task. Solesmes, as we have seen, was almost wholly occupied with the reconstruction and presentation of the ancient chant, but lengthy works of scholarship were also carried through, such as the critical edition of the works of John of St Thomas. At Ligugé, the home of the scholarly *Revue Mabillon*, much work has been done on monastic history. Farnborough in England was for some forty years a centre of learning; more recently, Clervaux in Luxembourg, founded in 1909–10 by the exiled monks of Glanfeuil, was able, soon after the First World War, to supply a community for the abbey of St Jerome, with the task of working on the critical text of the Latin Vulgate (1932).

Beuron, at first greatly influenced by Solesmes, became a centre of liturgical and historical study, and of several enterprises such as the great edition of the *Vetus Latina*, the pre-Vulgate Bible of the west. The congregation of Beuron may also justly take credit for the early fame of Maredsous, which in the years before the First World War harboured a constellation of scholars. Abbot Chapman, then a monk of the house and later (1929–34) abbot of Downside, was wont to remark that there were only two-and-a-half learned Benedictine abbeys – Maredsous, Farnborough and Downside (the half). In the interval between the wars, the other houses of the Belgian congregation acquired high reputations; several of them are the homes of liturgical, theological and historical periodicals, and at St Pierre de Steenbrugge a vast enterprise has begun in the *Corpus Christianorum*, which aims at presenting, in 120 volumes, a new critical text of the writers printed in Migne's great collection, together with works of these and other authors omitted by Migne.

The English congregation has been largely determined in its work by its early history. This, as we have seen, was deeply involved in the missionary needs of England in the Penal days, and in the educational demands of the English Catholics, who, if they wished for Catholic schooling for their children, could only find it in the religious houses abroad. All the English houses (save for the recently affiliated Buckfast) have been and are committed to these two forms of work, both of which have become more absorbing and demanding than could have been foreseen even as recently as eighty years ago. The schools in particular, which were originally small boarding houses, and which as recently as 1900 contained less than one hundred boys, very few of whom proceeded to university, grew, first with the growth of the well-to-do Catholic population of England, and latterly with the enormous growth of all secondary education, into large public schools of five hundred or more boys between the ages of fourteen and eighteen, with all the apparatus of laboratories, athletics and educational and recreational specialities that is demanded today of schools of the first rank. This presents a monastic community with problems and stresses that could not have been imagined a century ago, and it cannot be said that answers have been found to them. Yet another problem has been set for the parishes by the multiplication of churches and Mass-stations, and with the demands and mobility that are now expected of parish clergy. The quiet country presbytery of the nineteenth century, with a rural flock of families traditionally Catholic working on the estate of a country squire, has been replaced by a merger of two or more parishes, with other scattered gatherings on Sundays, to which clergy with cars travel, often collecting children by the dozen on their round. A community such as Ampleforth (Yorkshire, England), 150 strong, divided almost equally between staffing a school of 700 and a preparatory school nearby, and serving some twenty-five parishes, many of them large and in urban areas, scattered about Yorkshire, Lancashire, Cumberland and south Wales, has clearly monastic and spiritual problems as well as very great organisational tasks, and the abbot has a very different family to deal with than the household of the rule of St Benedict.

Similar difficulties are facing many north American abbeys. Here St John's Abbey, Collegeville, has a community double that of Ampleforth. Its dependent houses, ranging from the Bahamas to Tokyo, can care for themselves, but the abbot has to deal with monks running a large school, a university, parishes and mission stations in many different States. Here the experiment has been made of a prior, the abbot's lieutenant, who acts as a kind of vicar-general, visiting regularly all the monks living outside the monastic complex, but such an arrangement implies difficulties of its own. The two American congregations, indeed, are, like every widespread institute in the USA, coming to difficult cross-roads one after another, with large numbers threatening to fall into dis-array, not fully certain of their goal and so, like an army, unwilling to divide their forces in face of an enemy.

Finally, there are the congregations and houses in missionary work. They have practical problems which include the problem of survival in the guise of exhibits from an era of colonisation and western predominance. Will they be granted the time to establish firm traditions among the native population and with customs attuned to an African or Asian culture, or will they become extinct before the monastic life has taken a form permanently acceptable to non-Europeans? Consultations between monasteries in different territories have suggested that a completely vernacular liturgy with vernacular chant and gestures will be a necessity, and in fifty years time what will the name of St Benedict mean in central Africa? But meanwhile, till the deluge comes, the missionary monks have a life of austerity and rewarding work. They themselves, though of set purpose following a life far removed from that of the monastery

The refectory of Maredsous Abbey, where over one hundred monks are engaged in teaching a boarding school, in literary and liturgical work, and in giving retreats and conferences. Placed here among pages discussing modern monastic stresses and distresses, the picture might seem to be a silent question – how numerous, and of what kind, will be the monks of the future?

of the popular imagination, are perhaps less beset by problems from the new world of questioning and self-criticism than those living in Europe or north America.

It is these latter that the winds of change are buffeting in different ways. Those who live a stable, cloistered, liturgical life, in an age which has been shedding its traditions and its conventions, along with its sense of security and (on another level) its sense of mystery, are assailed with doubts as to the value, or indeed the psychological feasibility, of a liturgical, secluded monastic life at the present day. Some, on the other hand, who are deeply committed to active undertakings, a school or a group of parishes, question both the relation of that work to the rule they profess, and the possibility of retaining the modicum of monastic usage that has remained in their life. They are, many of them, in a difficult position for any discussion of principles, save the basic principles of the spiritual life. On the one hand it is very clear that their daily life, year in, year out, is not precisely that of the rule of St Benedict to which they take their vows. They have not even the support of their constitutions or declarations on the rule, for these are for the most part ambiguously silent as to the details and conditions of their teaching or pastoral work. On the other hand the work is there to hand, accepted long since in the past and fruitful in its own way, and who can say how fruitful and necessary in the near future.

At the end, an historian who has long pondered the problems that monks have faced in all ages, and that face them with painful insistence today, may be allowed the following observations.

First, that all monastic institutes must, as the fathers of the Second Vatican Council declared, seek guidance in their rule and the spirit of their founder. This, in the case of Benedictine and Cistercian monks, implies a return in spirit to the essential teaching of the ancient monks, as reflected in observant communities of all sub-

sequent ages. It implies also a careful following of the rule of St Benedict, not necessarily in all its liturgical or penal or social details, but assuredly in its essential spiritual teaching, which alters not with the ages. This, if any other, has been tried and approved by innumerable saints, and accepted and recommended by popes and synods and theologians times out of mind. No alleged need for *aggiornamento* and adjustments to modern ways of thinking can absolve those who would be faithful Benedictines from following Benedict's rule in its basic teaching. They do not depart from the rule by discontinuing corporal punishment and imprisonment for serious faults, nor by permitting a free use of the baths of the modern world.[29] They do not depart from the rule by reasoned and moderate changes in details of the liturgy, diet and domestic arrangements, for the author of the rule himself envisages such changes.[30] But they would depart from it by any derogation from its assertion of grave spiritual and monastic principles: absolute community and non-possession of all material things; absolute equality and uniformity as the norm for all duties and obligations, tempered only by the decision of authority on personal needs and abilities; residence in the monastery and within monastic observance not only 'for life' as a canonical status, but physically and with only rare and exceptional absence; silence at fixed times and places, and the absence of social contacts, pastimes and literature such as would seriously blunt the mind and its taste for spiritual things; obedience not only to the specific personal directions of the abbot, but to the spiritual discipline implied in the vow (*conversio morum*) of striving for an ever-deepening love and service of God.[31]

A monastic life according to the rule will imply that a considerable portion of the day be spent in liturgical service in choir, and in private prayer and spiritual reading. As we have seen, the monks of medieval Europe for many centuries made of liturgical prayer the *raison d'être* of their institute; their praise and intercession was that of their whole society. This way of acting did not precisely 'break' the rule of Benedict in a spiritual sense, but they certainly inflated part of its programme at the expense of other parts, and the retreat from this extreme, first by Cîteaux and later by almost all Benedictines, was in itself a return to earlier tradition. But to reduce the directly spiritual occupations of the day beyond a certain limit – a limit higher than that normal for devout priests or 'active' orders – would be to harm the monastic life irreparably. To say that all work is prayer, or that work done with and for others is of more spiritual worth than lengthy prayer, is to use fair-sounding phrases to cover a retreat from the one thing necessary, the direct adoration of the unseen God.

There remains the difficulty – the supreme difficulty in the modern world – of finding a work, a serious work, which at one and the same time can occupy several hours daily and yet not encroach upon the spiritual duties and atmosphere of the monastery so as to change it into a college of hard-working priests or religious who have only relatively few directly spiritual duties to perform in the day.

Three kinds of work would seem to fulfil these conditions. There is, first, the Cistercian work of farm and garden, in which the most exacting and physically laborious tasks are performed by brothers, leaving administration, craft work and straightforward manual work to the monks. This remains perhaps the best of all ingredients in monastic 'work'. For long, while the spirit of La Trappe prevailed, the Cistercian vocation was extremely exacting, both physically and psychologically. It is now once more truly traditional, an austere life, with physical work as an element, but with allowances also for study and learning.

Second, there is the less austere Benedictine regime with a mixture of literary work of all kinds together with a certain admixture of physical and manual occupation. While it is true that the number of scholars in the population of any country is small, and that as a class they are not notably spiritual, yet modern and even very recent experience has shown that a large community enterprise, such as the edition of a biblical or other important text, or co-operative work on a dictionary or a periodical, can give varied employment ranging from exact textual criticism to the practical and even manual work of preparing for press or printing, and work of this kind, efficiently planned, can be taken up for a few hours each day and adjourned without difficulty. A novice for such a community, which would also be a centre for retreats and religious conferences, would not need to be a potential scholar, but he would have to decide, as part of his noviciate, whether he could be content with one or other of the various occupations of the house.

Third, there is the missionary abbey. This, in suitable conditions, is a traditional and excellent work, if it is remembered that the primary duty of such a community is to be monks, in a home of public and private prayer and Christian virtue, and to influence apostolic work primarily by prayer and example, leaving to others the bulk of the active duties of teaching and preaching to those without. In such conditions the Cistercians have remained successfully within the monastic limits. Not all Benedictine houses have done so, or have aimed at doing so.

There remain the occupations of teaching and of parochial work. The staffing of an episcopal seminary, or of the theological faculty of a university would not seem to be of itself incompatible with the monastic life, if wisely ordered, though here again the question of recruitment might bring difficulties to a moderately sized monastery. More questionable is school teaching. It is difficult to see how the running of a large school, educating boys for university and the professions or business life can be reconciled in the modern world with the monastic vocation. Until about a century ago schools of this type were few and relatively small. The education given was mainly classical and literary, making relatively modest demands upon the teachers, and all games and interests were domestic and inexpensive. Moreover, the church, whether on the defensive or in the position of an establishment, still favoured a conservative, pietistic training which did not differ greatly from that the monks themselves received. Now, in Europe and America, and nowhere more than in England, the whole conception and scope of education have changed. The schools are large, and a number of monks must be regularly absent from many conventual duties, unless the monastic time-table is dislocated and to a certain extent deformed. The masters must immerse themselves in the subjects taught to the higher classes, they must take an interest in athletics of all kinds, and in the political and cultural interests of the world, in order to be able to meet their pupils on an equality and influence their education. Moreover, a schoolmaster's life, with its alternation of absorbing and exhausting duties in term-time, and reaction and lack of mental and spiritual energy in vacations, is at variance with monastic tranquillity.

Still less can permanent absence from the monastery as a priest with cure of souls provide the framework of a monastic life. This is not to decry the pastoral life, or its immense spiritual possibilities. But it is not in itself a monastic life for one with a monastic vocation, and the fact that individuals preserve some monastic practices together with spiritual zeal is no argument for confusing two different ways of life. And to those who urge the extreme importance of the pastoral life in the modern world, it may be answered that in the pastoral work of the church direct activity is not all. Christ himself, with a direct reference to the harvest field of souls, put prayer as the agency that sets in motion missionary work.

An answer to the questionings of today might be for what is now the Benedictine monastic body to recognise – not necessarily by any canonical division – that it embraces two large groups: those who retain the retired, liturgical and 'monastic' life of the rule of St Benedict and ancient tradition, and those who, while retaining the rule as a spiritual document, organise their life of prayer and work on what resembles the fashion of the regular canonical orders. A life of this kind could only be secured by a constitutional framework more precise and realistic than those which at present obtain in most monastic congregations. This would on the one hand clearly establish an adequate measure of observance and discipline, and on the other take note of both the legitimate demands and the inevitable spiritual difficulties of a schoolmaster's or a missionary priest's life, and would subordinate all activities not nominally but precisely to a single control, that of the abbot or prior. Such a code would demand for its making something of the mingled spiritual and practical wisdom of the rule itself.

We have passed beyond the limits of our brief in the last few pages, in the conviction that the monastic life has a future as well as an historical past. It has for more than seventeen centuries had a notable place in the life of the church. So far as we can judge it will not attain, in the foreseeable future, as it attained in the third century, in the sixth century, and again in the eleventh and twelfth centuries, to a religious, economic and social influence of the first importance in the life of both church and society. But it will remain as a Christian way of life for a greater or smaller number of individuals, with a significance greater than its numerical strength, and if a particular generation (even though it be our own) destroys it or disfigures it, it will return again when saints arise to show its nobility to the modern world.

Notes

All translations are by the author, unless otherwise stated.

1. Matt. xix 21.
2. Matt. xix 12.
3. See especially I Cor. vii 7, 30.
4. *Western Asceticism* (Library of Christian Classics, XII), London, 1958, p. 57. trans. Owen Chadwick, as also in three following quotations.
5. *Ibid.*, 79.
6. *Ibid.*, 105–6.
7. *Ibid.*, 142.
8. Cassian, *Conferences* I 199–200 (Chadwick, *Western Asceticism;* but author's translation).
9. St John of the Cross, *Maxims* (trans. E. A. Peers, *Works of St John of the Cross*, London, 1953, III 230; the original is numbered 236 in the critical text of Ph. Chevallier): 'Whatever thought of ours is not centred upon God is stolen from him.'
10. A Celtic poem from Connaught *c.*670, trans. by Professor James Carney, in L. Bieler's *Ireland, Harbinger of the Middle Ages*, London, 1963, 59. Quoted by kind permission of Professor Bieler.
11. It is now generally accepted that the *Rule of the Master* was composed in central Italy, *c.*530. Edited and trans. into French by Dom A. de Vogüé, 3 vols, Paris 1964–5.
12. *Rule of St Benedict, locc. cit.* For editions see Bibliography.
13. Bede, *Lives of the Abbots*, London, *Everyman* edition, 354–5; Latin original ed. C. Plummer, Oxford 1896, in *Baedae Opera*.
14. Letter of Boniface to the whole English race (AD 725), trans. D. Whitelock, *English Historical Documents*, London, 1955, I 748. This letter is No. 46 in M. Tangl, *Monumenta Germaniac Historisa Epistolae Selettae* I (1916).
15. Peter Damian, *Epistolae* vi 5 in Migne, *Pat. Lat.* cxlv col. 380.
16. *Udalrici Constitutiones* i 18 in Migne, *Pat. Lat.*, cxlix col. 668.
16a. Until about 1100 the term 'monk' was applied without distinction to all religions. Then the new body of Cîteaux who wore undyed woollen habits, were called 'white' monks, as opposed to the traditional 'black' monks. 'Benedictine' was a later name (1300).
17. *Rule* ch.1. 'Hermits . . . who . . . after long trial in a monastery . . . are

capable of the solitary warfare of the desert.' Ch. 73. 'Accomplish first this elementary rule for beginners . . . and then shalt thou attain to the greater heights [of the Fathers of the desert.]' It is perhaps significant that these two passages are placed, the one at the very beginning, the other at the very end, of the Rule.

18. *Exordium Parvum*, ed. J. Van Damme, in *Documenta pro Cisterciensis Ordinis Historiae ac Juris studio*, Westmalle 1959, 7.

19. See Bernard, *Apologia ad Willelmum*, c. xii 28, 29 (Migne, *Pat. Lat.* clxxxii coll. 914–6).

20. Suger, *De rebus in sua administratione gestis* (ed. E. Panofsky,) Princeton, 1946, 63–7.

21. Bernard, letter 106.

21a. These (canon=rule) were clerics following a rule, usually less severe than that of the monks.

22. Bernard, letter 64.

23. Ailred, *Speculum Caritatis* (*The Mirror of Friendship*) I 17. in Migne, *Pat. Lat.* cxcv 563.

24. Ailred, *De spirituali amicitia* (*On spiritual friendship*), I in Migne, *Pat. Lat.* cxcv 661.

25. Walter Daniel, *Vita Ailredi* xxxi, ed. Powicke (Nelson's Medieval Classics), London, 1950, p. 50.

26. I owe this saying, of Vladimir *c.* 1240, to Professor D. Obolensky.

27. For the time-table of the Rule, see E. C. Butler, *Benedictine Monachism*, 275–88; cf. Berlière, *L'Ascése Bénédictine*, Paris, 1927, 51–2, and P. Schmitz, art. Benoît, S., in *Dictionnaire de Spiritualité*. For Lanfranc, see *The Monastic Constitutions of Lanfranc*, ed. D. Knowles, London, 1951. For the time-table of the Congregation of France, I am indebted to the Rt Rev. Abbot A. Sillem. of Quarr abbey, and for that of Moint St Bernard, to the Rev. Fr Basil Morison, O.C.R.

28. In this chapter I have drawn heavily on Peter Anson, *The Call of the Cloister*, 2 ed., London, 1964.

29. Rule, ch. 37. 'Let the use of baths . . . be granted rarely (*tardius*) to the healthy and young monks'. The baths in question were probably a version of the elaborate hot-cold Roman bath.

30. Rule, ch. 18. 'If anyone dislikes this arrangement of psalms, let him

follow one which he thinks better ... provided the whole psalter is recited every week.' Benedictine and Cistercian monks of today are availing themselves of this permission while neglecting the proviso. Ch. 39. If the work is heavy, the abbot may increase the measure of food. Ch. 55. 'The clothing shall be adapted to the situation and climate of the house.'

31. *Abolition of ownership* ch. 33. 'This vice is to be cut out of the monastery by the roots'. *Equality* ch. 3 'All in all matters must follow the Rule'; ch. 2 'Whether serf or freeman, we are all one in Christ and bear an equal obligation of service under one Lord.' *Residence in monastery* Prologue: 'Persevering in the monastery till death.' Cf. the vow of stability, ch. 58. *Silence* ch. 6 'By reason of the great worth of silence, permission to speak shall rarely be granted.' *Withdrawal from the world* ch. 66. 'Let there be no need for monks to go abroad, for this is wholly contrary to their soul's good.' Ch. 4 'The monks' workshop is the enclosure of the monastery.' ch. 67 'Let no one tell another anything he may have seen or heard outside the monastery, for this is a frequent cause of disaster.'

Some statistics

Monastic numbers of the present day cannot easily be presented for purposes of comparison, as it is not always clear what categories should be, or have been, included in the total. The addition or omission of postulants, novices, oblates and lay-brothers can make a considerable difference to the total, and even the official *Annuario Pontificio* (Vatican City) depends on what returns the editor has used, and there are sometimes gaps in the figures. Moreover the number of houses, and of monks in each house, may vary considerably from year to year. Thus it would seem that the number of Cistercians (Reformed) in America fell by nearly five hundred in the period 1962–67. What follows is based chiefly on the current *Annuario Pontificio* and private information from reliable authorities.

Benedictine Confederation This consists of 17 Congregations, with about 12,070 monks. The Congregations largest in order of size are:

	independent houses	monks
American Cassinese	15	2000
Subiaco	47	1864
St Ottilien	11	1256
Beuron	9	1000
French	23	994
American–Swiss	9	963
English (including USA houses)	10	571

Note The larger number per house of the German abbeys and to a lesser extent those of USA are due to the large numbers of brothers. The English figures are official. The Olivetans (25 and 263) and the Vallombrosans (8 and 135) till recently separate orders, are included in the grand totals above. The Silvestrines (21 and 214) and Camaldolese (10 and 260) are still separate and are not included.

Cistercians of Common Observance	51 abbeys	1665 religious
Cistercians of the Reform (sometime Trappists)	80 abbeys	3770 religious
Carthusians (1957)	17 houses	688 religious

For purposes of comparison it may be noted that there were in 1960: 49,600 Franciscans (OFM 26,500; OFM Cap. 15,600; OFM Conventuals 7,500), 34,700 Jesuits and 9,500 Dominicans in the R.C. Church.

Bibliography

General

The most informative work on particular topics, places and persons may often be found in the encyclopedias or dictionaries such as: *The New Catholic Encyclopedia* (1967), the *Dictionnaire d'archéologie chrétienne et de liturgie*, the *Dict. d'histoire et géographie ecclésiastiques*, the *Dict. de droit canonique*, and the *Dict. de Spiritualité*.

M. Heimbucher, *Die Orden und Kongregationen der katholischen Kirche*, 2 vols 2 ed. Paderborn, 1933–4. Inclusive, factual, valuable, but occasionally uncritical; no recent edition.

P. Cousin, *Précis d'histoire monastique*, Paris, 1956. Rich in information, and quite invaluable for the student, despite numerous small inaccuracies of dates, names, spelling, etc.

P. Schmitz, *Histoire de l'ordre de S. Benoît*, 7 vols, Maredsous, 1942–56. English translation of early vols, London 1950; German translation, Zûrich, 1946 – Runs from St Benedict to 1950. The only historical survey. Entirely reliable, but necessarily somewhat superficial.

H. Leclercq, *L'ordre bénédictin*, 2 ed. Paris, 1943.

U. Berlière, *L'ordre monastique*, Maredsous, 1923. From St Benedict to Cistercians (inclusive). A brilliant feat of compressed fact and reflective comment.

S. Hilpisch, *Geschichte des Benediktinischen Mönchtums*, Freiburg–i.B., 1929, The standard work in German.

C. Butler, *Benedictine Monachism*, London, 1919, 2 ed. reprinted Cambridge, 1961. French transl. *Le monachisme bénédictin*, Paris, 1924. From St Benedict to twentieth century. The only work combining historical information with critical assessment; very readable and still without rival.

Early Eastern

K. Heussi, *Der Ursprung des Mönchtums*, Tübingen, 1936.

M. Viller, *La spiritualité des premiers siècles chrétiens*, Paris, 1930. German translation with additions, M. Viller, K. Rahner, *Askese und Mystik in der Väterzeit*, Freiburg–i–B., 1939.

D. J. Chitty, *The Desert a City*, Oxford, 1966.

O. Chadwick, *Western Asceticism*, (includes Fathers of Desert and Cassian), London, 1958.

W.R.Lowther Clarke, *St Basil the Great*, Cambridge, 1913.
The ascetic works of St Basil, London, 1925.

A.de Mendieta, *L'ascèse monastique de S. Basile*, Maredsous, 1949.

A.J.Festugière, *Les moines d'Orient*. II. Les moines de la région de Constantinople, Paris, 1961.

Early Medieval and Celtic

O.Chadwick, *John Cassian*, Cambridge, 1950, 2 ed. 1968.

L.Gougaud, *Christianity in Celtic Lands*, London, 1932; an improved version of *Les chrétientés celtiques*, Paris, 1911.

J.Ryan, *Irish Monasticism*, Dublin, 1931. Still the best work.

L.Bieler, *Ireland, Harbinger of the Middle Ages*, London, 1963.

K.Hughes, *The Church in early Irish society*, London, 1966.

Saint Benedict and his Rule. Europe 600–1100.

R.Hanslik, *Benedicti Regula*, Vienna, 1960. Elaborate apparatus, but received with no great enthusiasm. An *index verborum*=a concordance.

P.Schmitz, *La Règle de S.Benoît*, 2 ed., Maredsous, 1958. With French translation.

J.McCann, *The Rule of St Benedict*, with English translation and notes, London. The best English version, with helpful comment.

For the *Regula Magistri*, see M.D.Knowles, *Great Historical Enterprises*, London, 1963, pp. 139–95.

J.M.Clark, *The Abbey of St Gall*, Cambridge, 1926.

A.H.Thompson and others, *Bede: his Life, Times and Writings*, Oxford, 1935.

W.H.Levison, *England and the Continent in the Eighth Century*, Oxford, 1946.

S.J.Crawford, *Anglo-Saxon influence on Western Christendom, 600–800*, Oxford, 1933, reprinted Cambridge, 1966. Short but excellent.

Sankt Bonifatius, Fulda, 1954. Essential for its subject.

C.H.Talbot, *The Anglo-Saxon missionaries in Germany*, London, 1954.

E.de Moreau, *Histoire de l'Eglise en Belgique*, I, Brussels 1945.

F.Prinz, *Frühes Mönchtum in Frankenreich*, Munich-Vienna, 1965. Comprehensive and exhaustive, with complete bibliography.

N.Hunt, *Cluny under St Hugh,* 1049–1109, London, 1967.

D.Knowles, *The Monastic Order in England,* 2 ed., 1963. Includes chapters on European monachism.

Europe 1100–1500

L.Lekai. *Les Moines blancs*, Paris, 1957. An expanded and improved version of *The White Monks*, Okauchee, Wisconsin, 1953.

E.Vacandard, Vie de S.Bernard, 2 vols, Paris, 1895–7. Frequently revised and reprinted, and still fundamental. No English translation.

St Bernard, *Letters*, trans. B.Scott-James, London, 1953.

T.Merton, *The Last of the Fathers*, New York, 1954.

D.Knowles, 'Cistercians and Cluniacs', in *The Historian and Character*, Cambridge, 1963, 50–75.

W.Daniel, *Vita Ailredi*, ed. and trans. F.M.Powicke, London & Edinburgh, 1950.

M.Thompson, *The Carthusian Order in England*, London, 1930.

J.Leclercq, *L'Amour des lettres et le désir de Dieu*, Paris, 1957. English translation *The Love of learning and the desire for God*, Fordham, USA, 1960. German translation *Wissenschaft und Gottverlangen*, Düsseldorf. Perhaps the most notable of this writer's many excellent books.

J.Leclercq and others, *Histoire de la Spiritualité Chrétienne*, vol. 2, *La Spiritualité du Moyen-Age*, Paris, 1961. English trans. in progress.

D.Knowles, *The Religious Orders in England*, 3 vols., Cambridge, 1948–59.

Byzantium and Russia

Cambridge Medieval History vol. IV part 2, Cambridge, 1967. Full bibliography.

I.Smoltsch, *Russisches Mönchtum*, 988–1917, Würzburg, 1953. Full bibliography.

Post-Reformation monasticism

P.Schmitz, *Histoire* as above.

T. Ruinart, *Mabillon*, ed. Maredsous, 1933.

H. Leclercq, *Mabillon*, 2 vols, Paris, 1953–7.

M. D. Knowles, 'The Maurists', in *Great Historical Enterprises*, London, 1963, 34–62, and 'Jean Mabillon', in *Journal of Ecclesiastical History* x (1959), reprinted in *The Historian and Character*, Cambridge, 1963, pp. 213–39.

H. Bremond, *L'Abbé Tempête* (A. de Rancé), Paris, 1929. English translation *The Thundering Abbot*, London, 1931. An antidote to this book may be sought in A. D. Luddy, *The real De Rancé*, London, 1931, or A. Cherel, *Rancé*, Paris, 1930.

For the suppression and destruction in late eighteenth-century France, see Fliche & Martin, *Histoire de l'Eglise*, vol. xx, and P. Cousin, *Précis d'Histoire monastique*, 478–85.

For the nineteenth and twentieth centuries the best guides are the 1907 and 1967 *Catholic Encyclopedias*.

Monastic life and Spirituality

C. Butler, *Benedictine Monachism*, as above.

G. Morin, *L'idéal monastique*, 3 ed., Maredsous, 1921. English translation 1914; German, 2 ed., *Mönchtum und Urkirch*, Sainte Odile, 1944.

U. Berlière, *L'ascèse bénédictine*, Maredsous, 1922.

L. Bouyer, *Le sens de la vie monastique*, Turnhout 1950. English translation *The Meaning of the Monastic Life*, by K. Pond, London, 1955.

La spiritualité de Cîteaux, Paris. English translation, *The Cistercian heritage*, London, 1958.

C. Marmion, *Christ idéal du moine* (numerous edd.). English translation, *Christ the ideal of the monk*. See also R. Thibaut, *Dom Colomba Marmion*, Maredsous, 1953.

Monastic Architecture

M. Aubert, *Architecture cistercienne en France*, 2 vols., Paris 1947.

H. P. Eydoux, *L'architecture des églises cisterciennes d'Allemagne*, Paris, 1952.

M. D. Knowles and J. K. St Joseph, *Monastic Sites from the Air*, Cambridge, 1952.

Acknowledgments

Acknowledgment – further to any made in the captions – is due to the following for illustrations (the number refers to the page on which the illustration appears): Frontispiece, 38, 111, 216, 220 Leonard von Matt; 17 Roger Wood; 18 Louvre, Paris; 20–1 Scala Fotos, Florence; 28 Irish Tourist Office; 47 Mediaeval Academy of America; 56, 59 Bodleian Library, Oxford; 60, 86, 188 J. K. St Joseph, Cambridge University Collection; 63, 64, 101 (bottom), 137 138, 185 Alinari; 67 Roger Viollet; 76 Sociedad Arqueologica Luliana; 80, 173 Jean Roubier; 85 Metropolitan Museum, New York; 91 Niedersächsische Landesgallerie, Hannover; 99 Edwin Smith; 101 (top), Photo Yan; 102 Trinity College, Cambridge; 116 Kupferstichkabinett der Oeffentlichen Kunstsammlung Basel; 125, 140, 145, 153 British Museum; 131, 167 Novosti Press Agency; 150, 162 Giraudon; 163 Museo de Bellas Artes de Sevilla; 166 Museum of the History of Art, Zagorsk; 174 De Glau Studio, Penn., USA; 203 Bill Hedrich, Hedrich-Blessing; 239 Belgian State Tourist Office.

The maps were drawn by Design Practitioners Ltd.

Index